Operation Redemption

A Vision of Hope
In an Age of Turmoil

George Trevelyan

STILLPOINT PUBLISHING | 1985
WALPOLE, NEW HAMPSHIRE

This book is manufactured in the United
States of America. It is designed by
James F. Brisson, cover art by William Giese
and published by Stillpoint Publishing,
Box 640, Meetinghouse Road, Walpole, NH
03608.

Published simultaneously in Canada by
Fitzhenry & Whiteside Limited, Toronto.

Library of Congress Card Catalog Number:
85-50331
Trevelyan, George
Operation Redemption
ISBN 0-913299-17-0
0 9 8 7 6 5 4 3 2 1

Operation
Redemption

Contents

Foreword | By Kenneth Ring

W HEN I WAS INVITED to write a brief introduction for this new
American edition of *Operation Redemption*, I agreed immediately
and with enthusiasm for I am one of those—and we are many—
who believes that Sir George Trevelyan is one of those writers
with a planetary vision so profoundly stirring and important that
it deserves to reach the widest possible audience. And since
America seems to have a special role to play in bringing into manifestation what we persist in calling "the New Age" — for lack of
the ability to find a less tiresome phrase—I take a particular delight just in knowing that this seminal work is now being made
available to American readers.

If you are not already familiar with the work and writings of Sir
George, you should know that he ranks as one of the leading and
most compelling of the visionary architects of the New Age. Indeed, I think a good case could be made for the claim that Sir
George, now in his late seventies, might justly be regarded as
something of a patron saint of the New Age Movement. In any
case, in his educational endeavors throughout the years—and in
this book as well—he has certainly done as much as anyone to
articulate how we might best find our way to the future through
the developement of our spiritual potentials.

In *Operation Redemption*, Sir George offers his most recent for-
mulation of the coming planetary transformation. His world picture is rooted in a thoroughly holistic conception of life, in a frank
and convincing acknowledgment of the importance of the unseen

world and the notion of spiritual hierarchy, and in his inner certitude that "the coming of the Light" will—if we choose to align ourselves with it by deepening our own spiritual sensitivities—usher in an era of unprecedented human fulfillment, love and human brotherhood. Although cataclysmic events may be a part of this planetary transformation—indeed their very *possibility* appears to serve as an evolutionary catalyst—the extent of these changes can be significantly moderated by humanity's awakening to its inherent though long neglected spiritual resources. In the context of Sir George's thesis, however, the opportunities facing humanity between now and the end of the millennium are presented in a thoroughly empowering way. There is nothing dour here nor do images of doom predominate. Instead, Sir George outlines, as his subtitle promises us, "a vision of hope" — and it is an inspiring one indeed.

In bringing us this message of hope for the New Age, Sir George also takes us *back* to the ancient mystery teachings and to some of their modern hierophants. Thus, we are reminded of the contemporary relevance of the teachings of the Essenes, the Druids, and the Kahuna priests of Polynesia—as well as the writings of the great adept, Rudolf Steiner, who has had a great influence on Sir George's own thought. Esoteric Christianity and Eastern religions, especially Buddhism, are also explored here with penetrating insights into their significance for human transformation. There is of course much more in this book than I can adumbrate here, but I hope I have said enough about its contents to make it plain that *Operation Redemption* not only is a work of great prophetic significance, but that it is a book of wisdom as well. As such, I am sure you will find it deeply rewarding to study long after you have closed its covers for the first time.

Preface

THIS BOOK IS A SEQUEL to *A Vision of the Aquarian Age* published in the United States by Stillpoint Publishing in 1984. In that volume, discussion of the meaning and role of the Christ Impulse in our present age was somewhat deliberately suppressed for fear of drawing negative reactions in certain quarters. Many readers did, however, detect the omission, which stands like an empty hole in the argument of the book. In the present volume, I have tried to set this right. My hope, however, is that this in no way makes the book sectarian in its nature. It is concerned with the holistic world picture and its application to current problems, for axiomatically the Oneness Vision must touch and color every aspect of our living. It is concerned with the coming of the Light, the prospect of the redemption of mankind by the forces of higher intelligence in the living universe. This implies God is ubiquitous and in action. Furthermore, it implies the Blakean conception of a spiritual sun behind the physical sun, the focus of operation of the Elohim, the highest beings of spiritual Light. The Lord of all these is known in esoteric knowledge as the Christos and by other names in other religions.

But all recognize this overlighting source which can reach and be in personal touch with all souls of every race and creed, just as the physical sun warms all our bodies. Thus the concept of the Cosmic Christ is central to the holistic vision, and this has little to do with any sectarian thinking in any particular church. It must be a vital strand of our world view, and my hope is that it will not be taken as narrow dogma.

I have also referred not infrequently to the thinking of Rudolf Steiner, since this is the approach which I personally found most meaningful and inspiring. Again, my hope is that even for those who are not anthroposophists, these comments will help clarify basic issues in our dramatic time. Steiner achieved an intensification of intuitive thinking which enabled him to explore into the spiritual worlds in a manner consonant with scientific method, and to give us his findings in a great structure of clear thoughts which in no sense have a mediumistic character. Thus in our age of breakthrough, when spiritual knowledge is flooding from so many sources, the body of Steiner's thinking may stand as a kind of touchstone which can prove of deep significance to many different movements concerned with the spiritual awakening of the New Age.

Ours is an age of dramatic and even sensational change. The great theme is that there can be no renewal without a dying process, no death without resurrection. Thus events in the coming two decades are likely to be apocalyptic nature. This implies what I have called 'Operation Redemption,' a supreme hope that tribulation and cleansing change are a prelude to a new dawn.

George Trevelyan

Acknowledgments

For permission to use copyrighted material, the author gratefully makes the following acknowledgments:

To William Collins Ltd., for a passage from Teilhard de Chardin's *Le Milieu Divin.*

To Allen and Unwin Ltd., for a passage from Edward Carpenter's *Drama of Love and Death,* and for lines from a poem in Edward Carpenter's *Towards Democracy.*

To C.W. Daniel Ltd., for two short passages from Edmond Szekely's *Gospel of the Essenes.*

To Leonora Nichols, for three passages from her forthcoming book, *Within is the Fountain.*

Operation
Redemption

1 | Holistic Vision

THIS BOOK is an attempt to play with certain big thoughts and ideas. Play, indeed, light-heartedly, the heart filled with light, to dance with great Ideas, before the Lord. The ideas are powerful and serious, but need not be pompous or heavy. Have courage to think big thoughts, Our present world demands it of us.

And this in a world full of despair and gloom. How easy it is to be discouraged! Courage can seep away through our boots when we look at the prospects and listen to the 'media.' Violence, cruelty, breakdown of social structure and order; and behind all, the frightful and almost unimaginable prospect of nuclear disaster.

A mad, bad world indeed! We need encouragement.

This is our starting point. The situation facing us is in many ways so grim that we seem to be approaching the brink of catastrophe. Mankind is at the crossroads.

Unless there is some momentous change in human thinking, some great step forward into sanity, some turnabout in the very center of our consciousness, then we are faced with calamity. This is glaringly obvious.

Therefore, surely we are justified in trying to Think Big Thoughts.

We don't need to have an academic degree in philosophy. We can all lift and extend our thinking and try to look at our overwhelming problems from a cosmic viewpoint; look down on our beautiful planet from above in space; see it like the photographs on television, shining blue and silver and turning marvelously in the seas of space; then realize, as Edgar Mitchell did in his 'peak experience' as he came out from behind the Moon, that the Universe is a great continuum of consciousness and thought. It works as a great Oneness in celestial harmony. Our delicate, beautiful planet moves in its dance with its fellows around the source of our life, the radiant Sun.

Then realize that in all that harmonious movement and pattern there is one area deviating from the Divine Law, thrown into confusion and darkness. This is the human kingdom of emotion, desire and will. Planet Earth is darkened and confused and unhappy. We have inherited from our grandfathers a picture of man and the universe which admittedly swept away much old dogma but landed us into the present materialistic world picture. "Reductionist" it was called—a belief that the whole was no more than the sum of all its parts. We could thus by scientific investigation gradually explain every aspect of the workings of life until we had reduced it to a mechanism. When all was thus accounted for, we could see that there was no room for God, that He was no more than the word we gave to that which we had not yet explained.

Thus the marvelous human body came to be treated as a machine for which a spare parts service can be developed. Man was seen as essentially an accident of evolution, a chance concatenation of atoms brought together by natural selection. We discover a universe so huge and so old and apparently so completely indifferent to puny man that his life can have little meaning. And by a strange paradox, having (so he thought) discovered his total unimportance in a mechanistic universe, he feels himself fully justified in exploiting the planet for his own advantage and desire. What does it matter that we use up the Earth's resources? The Earth is surely dead mineral and can't feel. And anyway, death is the end, so "Let us eat, drink and be merry, for tomorrow we die."

But we should know and experience that in our time a turnabout in thinking is actually taking place. A wholly different World View is emerging, spreading and leavening our materialistic culture.

A great change in world view is emerging, which, if we grasp it, can lift and lighten our hearts with hope and even joy. This is being called the holistic world view. That wonderful word "holistic," first invented by General Smuts, links in derivation "wholeness", "holiness" and "healing".

The Whole is Holy. Healing is a restoring to Wholeness. We enter gropingly into a vast vision of the Oneness of All Life, and it is breath-taking. It is an inflooding of an understanding which will lift us right out of and beyond the materialistic, reductionist view of life. This is not to say that the previous thinking was wrong, as such. Thought is a great structure. It may be likened to a wall. The upper tiers of brick or stone rest on the foundation and all the intermediary tiers. Freud and Darwin brought about a revolution in thinking which swept away much outdated dogma and, on a certain level, revealed great truth. But no truth is final and absolute. We are called on perpetually to move forward. The earlier tiers or terraces are steps on which we can build ever greater structures. So we extend the viewpoint to see beyond what our great predecessors gave us.

To quote a fine passage from Earl Balfour:

> *Our highest truths are but half-truths;*
> *Think not to settle down for ever in any truth.*
> *Make use of it as a tent in which to pass a summer's night,*
> *But build no house of it, or it will be your tomb.*
> *When you first have an inkling of its insufficiency*
> *And begin to descry a dim counter-truth looming up beyond,*
> *Then weep not, but give thanks:*
> *It is the Lord's voice whispering,*
> *'Take up thy bed and walk'.*

So the Idea with which we are now engaged is the Oneness picture, the holistic world view which recognizes the sacredness of all life and sees that the whole is very much more than the mere sum of its parts.

"But I don't believe in God. If there's a God, how can he allow so much suffering and cruelty in his world? Since I can't see the spiritual world, how can I prove it exists?"

How easily and justifiably can this attitude be taken in our agnostic society. How lightly can we say, as sensible, practical men and women, *let us get on with our problems and not waste time in speculation about imponderables.* And yet, and yet . . . it is true enough that the Divine world cannot be proved to the cold rational intellect alone, but other ways to knowledge are emerging.

Let us make it quite clear from the first that what is written here is no dogma or doctrine which you are asked to believe. None of the great spiritual researchers has asked for *belief.* Rather they have invited *thought.* If you like these ideas, learn to hold them in your heart and mind without believing—or disbelieving. Look at life in the light of them, meantime reserving judgment. If they are true, they will draw to themselves an inner certainty as the days go by. If not, they will fall away and fade. Take this as a simple but very significant technique for exploring into realms where Truth cannot be weighed and measured and "proved." For Truth never constrains. It leaves you free to accept or reject. Yet recognize that we all have a power of apprehending an idea for its very beauty. We can grasp it out of the ether and take possession of it. *Oh, how lovely. That explains life. It must be true.* Not very scientific, and cold reason can all too easily come with its dampening and discouragement. But know that this experience is a first step in the developing of the faculties of higher perception of a realm of Ideas which cannot be immediately proven.

We do not need to try to disprove these things by argument. Most argument is a rather debased form of human exchange involving the attempt to shoot down the other fellow when he leaves a loophole with which we can disagree.

The great spiritual ideas are in a mysterious sense alive. To take them and dissect them by argument is like taking a flower or a butterfly and pulling it to bits. Imagine that an idea is a living creature, a being which can be loved and cherished. You are approaching a facet of the vast complex crystal of Truth, and you have seen it glint. Do not smash the crystal. Look—and listen. True conversation is a most wonderful thing, very different from argument and even discussion, in which the logical intellect is used to dissect and analyze. But "conversation," a "turning about together," is an almost magical process. Notice it. It is a condition of human exchange, between two or three or more of us, in which each is helping the others to grasp and see facets of the hovering crystal of Truth which has, almost like the Grail, descended from some higher realm to float over us, half perceived. The real "conversations" come unbidden, of their own accord, and withdraw when they so decide. We cannot hold them. They are an event which we must observe and respect. They leave us with a sense of melting in the heart, as if a Presence had been with us. We are more closely united with others because we have been overlighted by the great Being of Truth. "Where two or three are gathered together in My name, there am I in the midst of them."

Here truly we can dance with ideas, breathe in the light-filled air of intuition and imagination. We are learning to explore into the realm of the imponderables. Logical intellect alone, great though its achievements are, cannot enter this higher world of life. It is the more sensitive, feminine faculties of intuition that are called for and must be awakened.

Come back to our first point—the outer world is so cruel, so dangerous, so altogether ugly in many of its aspects, that we are fully justified in turning inwards to discover the magic gateway into the greater spiritual realms. By no means is this mere "escapism." It will turn out to be an essential process of lifting thinking and vision so that we may see our problems from a higher outlook point, setting them in the context of a cosmic consciousness.

Then our present troubles are seen as an aspect of a profound change, coming upon us to cleanse our polluted planet and bring renewal. The prospect brings supreme hope. It may even be that our present global problems are insoluble unless we achieve this widening of consciousness. Let us look at it, play with it, dance with it.

Let us begin by briefly stating the holistic world view. Remember; don't treat this as dogma to be believed. Keep thinking flexible; stand back and look at the Whole of which we are part.

This world picture is only new in the sense that it supersedes a materialist outlook to which it is alien and by which it has simply been forgotten and overlooked. It is as old as human thinking and flows through the great religions and cultures of the past. The development of acute intellectual self-consciousness has lost it to us. The reason for this loss is simple: the price we have had to pay for the developing of intellect, so essential for analyzing and controlling the physical world in a scientific age, is the atrophying of the organs of perception which enabled our ancestors to perceive the spiritual worlds and the realms of the elemental beings and nature spirits. Now, while retaining the clarity of intellectual observation, it becomes possible to expand consciousness into the Whole and so to blend thinking with the Oneness of the world process.

This is the beginning of a true science of the spirit.

Earth is experienced as indeed a living creature, an organism with, in a real sense, its own breathing, blood stream, heartbeat and glands, its skeleton and muscle, its life and thought. Mankind is integrally part of this living organism and is indeed an aspect of the thinking of the planet. The body is a sensitized point of earth; the mind is a bridging point that can reach up into the Cosmos. Mankind, the bearer of consciousness, the crowning point of evolution, is thus clearly seen as the steward of the planet. And what have we done with our stewardship?

You do not get a living organism in the midst of dead mechanism. We must feel for the tremendous conception of organism within greater organism. All is Life. Everything is in some sense imbued with life. All is thought in a vast continuum of consciousness. The human mind, in Woachi Brooke's phrase, is "a pulse of the eternal Mind, no less." Thus Earth, a living creature, is integrally part of the spiritual organism of the Solar System and that of the galaxy and so on, ad infinitum.

Thus the Whole is Holy. God is the name we give to the ineffable, unknowable First Cause, the Source. It, He/She, can no longer be left out from our world picture. The attempt by reductionist thinking to exclude the Creator can never satisfy the depths of human longing. As Pope put it in his *Essay on Man:*

> *All are but parts of one stupendous Whole,*
> *Whole body Nature is, and God the soul.*

Teilhard de Chardin as scientist and mystic has given us the beautiful concept of "complexification." It appears that atoms and cells have within them an inbuilt urge to complexify, thus evolving ever more complex organisms, and with each onward step is achieved a heightening of consciousness. Evolution reaches an intensely great complexity in the human brain, which is thus the bearer of self-consciousness on earth. He argues from this that the human monad, as an individual cell of the noosphere, must come together in yet greater complexification in closer grouping with others in an ultra-human blending, resulting in the inevitable upward step from individual self-consciousness. He writes, "We have glimpsed the marvels of a common soul." Here is the goal and purpose of the agelong experiment of creation. Indeed Teilhard sees this built-in urge within the cell as a proof of a purposive drive working through evolution.

To quote Pope again:

> *Mere storms casually together hurled*
> *Could ne'er produce so beautiful a world.*

For Man is a being,
> *God begotten, God companioned*
> *Forever Godward striving.*

Such a world view is, of course, not new. It is a fresh expression, suitable for our age, of the oldest truths held by all the great religions. Here are a few expressions from ancient scripture.

Taoism

> *There is a Spirit which was before the heavens and the earth were. It is the One dwelling in silence, beyond earthly forms, never-changing, omnipresent, inexhaustible.*
>
> *I do not know its name; but if I have to give it a name I call it Tao, I call it the Supreme.*
>
> *To go to the Supreme is a wandering, a wandering afar, and this wandering afar is a returning.*
>
> *Man on earth is under the law of earth. The earth is under the law of heaven. Heaven is under the law of Tao. Tao is under its own law.*
>
> *Lao Tzu. 600 B.C.*

Hinduism

> *There is a Light that shines beyond all things on earth, beyond us all, beyond the heavens, beyond the highest, the very highest heavens. . . . This is the light that shines in our heart.*
>
> *All the universe is in truth Brahman. He is the beginning and end and life of all. As such, in silence, give unto Him adoration.*

There is a spirit that is mind and life, light and truth and vast spaces. He enfolds the whole universe and in silence is loving all.

This is the Spirit that is in my heart, smaller than a grain of mustard seed, greater than the earth, greater than the heavens, greater than all these worlds.

He contains all works and desires, all perfumes and tastes.

This is the Spirit in my heart, this is Brahman.

To Him I shall come when I go beyond this life.

And to Him will come he who has faith and doubts not.

Chandogya Upanishad. 800 B.C.

Buddhism

Rouse thyself by thy Self, thy Spirit: train thyself by thy Self.

Thus under the shelter of thy Self and ever watchful, thou shalt live in supreme joy.

If a man conquer in battle a thousand and a thousand more, and another man conquer himself, this would be the greater warrior: because the greatest of victories is the victory over one's self.

Hebrew

In the beginning God created the heaven and the earth. And the earth was without form and void; and darkness was on the face of the deep. And the Spirit of God moved upon the face of the waters. And God said Let there be Light: and there was Light.

Genesis I.

Christian

In the beginning was the Word, and the Word was with God and the Word was God. The same was in the beginning with God. All things were made by him, and without him was not any thing made

*that was made. In him was Life, and the life was the light of men.
And the light shineth in the darkness and the darkness compre-
hended it not.*

John I.

Science

*The universe looks less and less like a great machine and more
like a great thought.*

*If the universe is a universe of thought, then its creation must
have been an act of thought. Indeed the finiteness of time and space
almost compel us, of themselves, to picture creation as an act of
thought. Modern scientific theory compels us to think of the Creator as working outside time and space, which is his creation, just as
an artist is outside his canvas.*

Sir James Jeans.

And now we may read Dr. Fritjof Kapra's remarkable book, *The
Tao of Physics*, to realize that the most advanced physicists are
now speaking essentially the same language as the mystics in revealing that all matter is energy and all energy ultimately a manifestation of a universe of consciousness.

To the eye of the mind emerges a world within and behind the
forms. From Divine Thinking, these myriad forms have emerged.
As they fade and die, the Being or Spirit within them is released
again to return to its source. So, behind the outer world is an
inner world, and the possibility of mind moving within and
within, to expand through into a realm beyond substance, a
world of infinity and eternity.

In Blake's words, the task is

*To open the Eternal Worlds, to open the Immortal Eyes Of Man
inwards into the Worlds of Thought; into Eternity Ever expanding
in the Bosom of God, the Human Imagination.*

Thus the human being provides the "bridging point" between the physical and ethereal worlds, between the field of gravity and its polar opposite which should be called levity.

Mind within us is one with Universal Mind. In our thinking, we can be one with the Ocean of Thought; in our feeling, the Ocean of Love can play through us; in our willing, an Ocean of Living Will can operate in the world of substance. There is an Ocean of Life which is God in Action. The essence of each of us, that which can say "I" to itself, is a droplet of this ocean, a spark of the Divine Fire. Since Life is inextinguishable, that spark of Being must be immortal and imperishable . . . (Don't believe, but take that idea into the heart and live *as if* you believed it.)

Shakespeare writes of "proud man . . . Most ignorant of what he's most assured,/His Glassy essence . . ." (Measure for Measure). For the Essence, there is no death, its survival is most assured. The outer forms, when they have done their service, can break down, dissolve, be metamorphosed. And indeed, the "dying" of the sheath is an essential process in the cycle of life. As Goethe wrote, "Nature invented death that there might be more life."

We grasp first the concept of the Oceans of Creative Life and Thought, there from the primal beginning yet weaving through all substance on a vibratory rate far higher than the dense vibrations of earth. With the creation of solid substance inevitably comes time as we know it; one thing must begin to happen after another. But in the beginning was Life, and "the Life was the Light of man." It is not the right question to ask: "When did Life begin?" Life always was. From the condensing of thought into substance comes the secondary condition of hardening which we call death. The world of free spirit dips down into the fascinatingly beautiful realm of matter, in order there to sojourn and operate, for the gaining of experience in a condition of temporary separation from the Source. Human birth is therefore to be seen as a kind of death, a descent into the prison or tomb of the body and personality and the five senses. This is a drastic limitation of a free-ranging spirit. "Death" must then in reality be more of a birth, a release from limitation back into the realms from which we came and to which we really belong. We are called on to take the step which reunites us with the Source. We are each the Prodigal Son, eating the husks with the swine until we "come to ourselves" and say "I will go back to my Father." And the Father sees us afar off and comes out with joy to meet us. This is the way home.

The materialistic outlook inevitably leads many people to a loss of the sense of meaning to life. What is it all about? With the holistic world picture we rediscover that, in a real sense, Man is the central purpose of it all. He appears as the great experiment of God. The Earth is the chosen training ground of the soul. We are here to experience separation from the Divine Will and thus to develop self-consciousness, ego-consciousness and the beginnings of free will in creative action. This inevitably allowed the right to err and deviate from the Law. Hence egoism and evil, which the last centuries have seen so strongly in the West. With egoism and desire come greed, rivalry, fear, hate and war—a deadly cycle. This is the Fall of man. Next must come his redemption so that creative free will can be used to the glory of God. The beginning of this process is now being experienced. One soul after another begins to recover the lost vision. We awaken, aghast, to what we have done to the planet through our neglected stewardship. We learn to see that we are each ambassadors of God who have forgotten the Lord to whom we are responsible. Mankind has been called the Tenth Hierarchy, "a little lower than the angels."

In George Griffiths' words:

> *Man, as nexus of two worlds*
> *stands poised at this mid-between*
> *on razor's edge*

gifted beyond angels
benizoned in light
and cast in the major role
could he but know it.

Certain high-level communications received by sensitives from spiritual sources have clearly stated that so long as man insists on trying to deal with his self-created problems on the assumption that the Earth is a dead mineral body in a mechanistic universe, he will never overcome and solve his difficulties. Human self-sufficiency is inadequate and the damage already too great. But if he can learn to see the Wholeness and attune to the Powers of the Living Oneness of which he is part, then nothing is insoluble. Here is the ignored factor in all of our ecological, economic and political efforts. Are we not to call on these forgotten allies for our salvation and redemption? Though invisible, this power is positive and operative. It is going into action, and the results of this will become increasingly apparent. We must wake up to the part we have got to play in this drama, in invoking and channeling the coming Light. This approach restores a sense of meaning to life and awakens in us a sense of urgency and of the dramatic nature of the time we live in. And it brings with it the supreme hope that after the tribulation will come a great renewal.

LOOK UP FOR YOUR REDEMPTION DRAWETH NIGH.

2 | The Quickening of the Spirit

THE NEW ERA will bring in, once again, the age-old wisdom which will release man from the scourge of disease; as he learns to tune in to the divine universe around him, he will find all that is needed to give him this power, but only to be reached as he understands his relationship to the divine whole.

These universal energies that are everywhere present are radiant pulsations of pure life or magnetic light that make up the body of the Universe of which the manifested self is an integral part.

You have but to draw upon these divine energies in order to restore that which has been harmed or to revitalize that which has been dulled and decimated by misuse or ignorance.

"I have come," He said, "to give thee Life, Life more abundant." He did not mean more material things or worldly pleasures but a greater sense of the divinity of Life and how to be a more vital part of it.

Man has forgotten that he is a creative expression of the Living Universe and, as such, a child of the Universal Presence within it. Understand these things, for man's purpose now is to move out into his divine Destiny and away from the disintegrating mooring to an old and dying world.

This inspired passage comes from a spiritual journal called *Within is the Fountain* by an American friend, Leonora Nichols. It gives us the direct application of the holistic vision and indicates the path of inner striving.

We watch and take part in a spiritual awakening which is surging forward on a broad front. We call it, loosely, the New Age Movement. The variety of its manifestation can be bewildering and sometimes rather "way-out," but every facet is the expression of the living Whole. Hence the great importance of the holistic world picture.

This world view implies that we are one with the Unity of All Life. We are not over against it, observing it. We are it. If once we can overcome the limitation of sense bound thinking, we discover that consciousness is potentially anywhere. Instantly, it can project itself to any part of the Universe. Thought moves farther than light, since it is instantaneous. Of course we need to learn the art and technique, for we are bogged down by the centuries of logical, rational thinking which assumes the limitations of gravity. But man is the bridging point between two worlds. We may be on the threshold of a wonderful transformation of mankind, an opening into new dimensions of consciousness which would be like the entry into a new Golden Age. Events are dramatic to a degree. Life is sensational, holding imminent possibility of transformation or catastrophe, or perhaps transformation *through* catastrophe if we have not the intelligence to stop doing those things which are rushing us towards the abyss. All our troubles may prove to be the birth-pangs of the new age. Earth is in labor, and just as the parents of a child a-borning will look with gladness and anticipation beyond the labor pains, so may we look forward to the bright morrow dawning beyond tribulation.

To see our present troubles in their true perspective, we must lift our thinking into the whole and view Planet Earth, time-ridden and embattled, from an eternal viewpoint. Think into the great sweep of Divine Creation.

First the Almighty Consciousness pours itself out into the nine Hierarchies of angelic beings (of which more later). Our picture must grasp the supreme concept that God creates the archetype of man "a little lower than the angels" at the outset of the whole process. Last to appear in physical embodiment through evolution of the vehicle which can carry soul and spirit, Man is first in Idea. It needs aeons of evolution to perfect the instrument. For Man is the great experiment of God, a creature who can carry the divine gift of free will. Within all his wonderful creation, God needs some point which can respond personally to Him. Trees and plants, rocks and animals can work to his Law, but the Creator must need a facet of his creation which can stand up to him as son to Father and become in time a companion and friend, and more exciting still, a co-creator. Man is that point in evolution where nature becomes self-conscious and reflective. He begins to create with his intelligence. We call this "Creation Mark II." Think of the enthralling prospect when from the spiritual worlds, the angelic beings look down and see the beginnings of free creativity upon Planet Earth. It implies that everything is moving up the evolutionary spiral towards ever-heightening consciousness and creativity, world without end. Glory be! The true human potential is unlimited, for man is a part of the structure of life and consciousness, reaching back and onward into the creative thinking of the Supreme Source, God the All-Knower.

The beautiful planet Earth is the chosen setting for this great experiment. Clearly it involved an element of gamble, since it meant that the human being must pass through acute self-consciousness and egoism, with the resultant opportunity to err out of greed and desire, before he discovers the real purpose of life on Earth. Hence the sorry condition which we have brought about on the planet and the need for a rescue operation.

For the Oneness picture implies that Earth is indeed a living organism within the greater organism of the solar system. The planets may be compared with the endocrine glands. If one of these tiny organs goes wrong, the health of the whole body is impaired. So it is with the body of the solar system. It works in harmony with the Divine Law, except where the errant stewards of Planet Earth, in reckless greed and ignorance, have polluted their planet and threaten to destroy life upon it. Thus the harmonious life of the whole is gravely disturbed. It is essential to the well-being of the whole that Earth should come into line, that the evil and darkness should be swept away and the darkened aura cleansed.

Human intellect and genius has now discovered that apparently solid matter is all energy and further has found how to harness this energy. But, morally and emotionally, mankind is still too immature to hold such godlike responsibility. He is still playing with toys, which was relatively harmless when it involved bows and swords, but will not do when he uses nuclear bombs and bacteriological weapons of war. Therefore, from out of the living body of the Universe must surely come a flooding of redemptive energy which will cleanse the planet. This stupendous event appears to be upon us, and the last quarter of the twentieth century is likely to be a time of profound transformation.

Thus, I have called this book *Operation Redemption*, implying that out of the vast continuum of consciousness an active impulse has been launched to transmute the evil. That this is actually happening there is much evidence. Here is another concept that we may take and live with, reserving judgment but watching life in the light of it. It would explain many of the strange events and trends in our time. It is a perfectly logical development, for we cannot expect the higher worlds to stand by and watch indefinitely while we pollute the planet to satisfy our own desire and avarice.

We have seen that Earth itself, our Mother Earth, is a living sentient creature. Is it not possible that she will react against parasite Man's raping of her? Perhaps some of the earthquakes and volcanic eruptions and atmospheric disturbances are really this slow creature shrugging off the irritant of Man with all his greedy pollution.

But central to the whole world picture is the concept of the human being as a creature of free will, the Divine experiment in developing what has been called the Tenth Hierarchy. Therefore, no divine intervention may deny human freedom. Thus we may not expect the forces of Light simply to take us over without our consent.

This implies the profound importance of human initiative in invoking the angelic energies and consciously offering a channel for their redemptive working. The dark forces striving to win the human soul have no compunction in taking possession. One thing the energies and beings of Light can do if mankind will not listen is to hit him with disaster and catastrophe. The holistic vision certainly shows us that there is no difficulty for the beings directing human destiny to stage events of a calamitous nature. Death, after all, is the great educator. In our death-ridden culture, the great step we have to take is to learn that the spiritual entity in us is immortal and cannot die. The outer sheath of the body may be destroyed to release the soul/spirit from its imprisonment in matter and form. We may accept these concepts intellectually, but it remains theoretical knowledge until we have experienced death personally, whether through the loss of a beloved friend or relative or the real facing of our own death.

Thus current events and the disturbances of our time may be seen as the prelude to Operation Redemption, before the ringing up of the curtain for the grandest opera ever staged. Such is the age we live in, and it is a privilege to be involved.

The difficulties facing everyone are such that it is all too easy to get bogged down in mundane worries and problems of survival and adjustment. How important, therefore, that we should entertain the tremendous concept of angelic energies, loving and beneficent but powerful, dedicated to the bringing of Earth life into harmony with the Divine Workings of universal life, and operative now on the supersensible levels, penetrating our consciousness, seeping through our whole society, activating and intensifying life energies within nature and even (as is suggested) speeding up the vibratory rate within all matter. This would mean that we are on the verge of a breakthrough into fourth-dimensional consciousness.

Such changes will be bewildering to those who are still tied to the materialistic interpretations of life and the universe. To those who can open consciousness to the spirit, all the dramatic events may bring a supreme hope of a transformation which, beyond tribulation, will lead to the birth of a new society. This is a source of excitement, expectation, anticipation and joy, which can enable us to ride out the times of difficulty.

The image comes of a dam beginning to leak. Efforts are made to stop the leaks by patching it up. But the trickles may grow into streams which will wash around all obstacles and undermine them, and the time may come when the dam breaks and the flood comes. If we can see the flood as the outpouring of the Waters of Aquarius and the Powers of the Transforming Spirit, then beyond tribulation will come the great renewal.

To those who say that this is airy stuff unrelated to the serious problems of our time and who ask for some real evidence, we could answer: "Circumspice." Really observe what is coming to birth already by way of a new compassion, cooperation, human sympathy and tolerance. It is being called the "Alternative Life-style." We are conditioned by the media today to look at the violence and cruelty and all the manifestations of despair and distortion of the human soul. But this is not the real news. Behind all breakdown and distress rises the sublime hope of God and the powers of Christ watching and acting. For may we not believe that God knows what He is about and bides His time, and that His timing is perfect? Considering the gravity of the alternatives, is it not valid to stake our bottom dollar on the possibility of changes sensational and dramatic indeed, but filled with the supremest hope that mankind has ever conceived?

To quote the quatrain from James Elroy Flecker:

> *Awake, awake, the world is young*
> *For all its weary years of thought,*
> *The starkest fights must still be fought,*
> *The most surprising songs be sung.*

3 | The Cosmic Christ in the New Age

THE COMING OF THE NEW AGE is heralded by a spiritual awakening which is to be distinguished from what has commonly been understood by the phrase "a religious revival." It has not grown out of the churches or conventional religions, though it can bring fresh ardor into every church. Yet this broad movement is truly religious in its nature in that it is a recognition of the stupendous Oneness of all life in its infinite diversity. All life is of God and everything is of Divine origin. Furthermore, there is the widespread conviction not only that higher worlds of spirit are a reality, but that a "pressure" from those worlds is breaking into our lives and lifting human consciousness in this very generation. Many great seers have foretold some great spiritual "crisis" or evolutionary turning point for mankind by the end of the twentieth century. This, in some way, must involve an expansion of consciousness to take in other dimensions of reality, for it becomes very clear that our earth-bound consciousness is by no means the only level that the human mind can experience.

The recognition that life is a Divine Oneness and that mankind is indeed one great family becomes an essential part of our world view. We can at least accept it intellectually and then, with the imagination, strive to understand the implication. We can recognize that "Spaceship Earth" is truly a living sentient being or creature of which we men are a part. Man is that point where evolution becomes conscious of itself. In us the planet can think towards God, who can experience Himself reflected in Man. We come to see that not only is the planet alive, but the whole Cosmos is in very truth shot through with creative intelligence and spirit from which all physical substance is derived. To quote R. M. Bucke from *Cosmic Consciousness* in speaking of the experience of mental illumination:

> *Like a flash there is presented to his consciousness a clear concep-*
> *tion (a vision) in outline of the meaning and drift of the universe.*
> *He does not come to believe merely; but he sees and knows that the*
> *Cosmos, which to the self conscious mind seems made up of dead*
> *matter, is in fact far otherwise—is in truth a living presence. He*
> *sees that instead of men being, as it were, patches of life scattered*
> *through an infinite sea of non-living substance, they are in reality*
> *specks of relative death in an infinite sea of life. He sees that the life*
> *which is in man is eternal, as all life is eternal; that the soul of man*
> *is as immortal as God is. He obtains such a conception of The*
> *Whole or at least of an immense Whole as dwarfs all conception,*
> *imagination or speculation springing from the belonging to ordi-*
> *nary self consciousness, such a conception as makes the old at-*
> *tempt mentally to grasp the universe and its meaning petty and*
> *ridiculous.*

Commenting on the awakening of our age, the late Tudor Pole, one of the great adepts of our period, wrote in his last book *Writing on the Ground:*

> *It is my belief that the "Revealer of the Word" (the Christos) for the*
> *historic times in which we now live, has already descended into the*
> *invisible spheres that surround our planet and that those with eyes*
> *to see and ears to hear, can begin to discern the Message he is*
> *bringing, even if the Messenger may not be clothed in form or out-*
> *wardly discernible. He will bring with him the inspiration and the*
> *spiritual impetus we need in order to lift human consciousness out*
> *of its present darkness into the Light of new Day. One thing is*
> *certain. If we are to equip ourselves to receive and understand the*

*Revealer, the coming Messenger from God, we must arouse our-
selves from sleep and prepare ourselves for this arrival.*

Who and what is the Christos? Clearly, an exalted being of
Light must overlight *all* mankind. He must illumine every race,
creed and nation. There can be nothing sectarian about Him.
Truth and Love must play down to every man, whether atheist or
believer. The great world religions need not merge and indeed
should not merge, for each of them carries a tremendous facet of
the Truth. But over all, a real and all-embracing world religion
could begin to appear in recognition of the Lord of Light, overlighting all mankind.

The name "the Christos" is the Greek term for this Exalted
Being of the Spiritual Sun. The worship of the Spirit of Light and
Truth is common to all the great religions which acknowledged
His approach to the Earth for the redemption of mankind, though
there was disagreement and uncertainty concerning the time and
nature of this deed of entry. To Christians, He is the Christ, but
clearly the present vision would lift us far above the sectarian
conflicts which have through history caused such bloodshed in
the name of Christian religion. We are dealing with concepts
which would renew and widen Christianity so that, veritably, the
coming of the New Age would be seen to include and express the
Christ Impulse for all mankind.

I choose to look at this through the idiom of the teachings of
Rudolf Steiner, since I am most familiar with his approach. I do
not think this will be essentially at variance with the teachings of
other great spiritual investigators. Steiner's clarity of perception
truly heralded the present awakening. Born in 1861 and dying in
1925, he was a great scientist who also from his youth possessed
complete clairvoyance, so that the reality of the spiritual worlds
was obvious to him. However, as a scientist, he saw that this
faculty must be transmuted into a thinking which was consonant
with scientific method. If Divine Intelligence was the creative

power behind all nature and life, then the human mind must be able so to lift its thinking that it could blend in consciousness with the world process. Then true investigation of higher knowledge by immediate experience would be possible. Truth would then be apprehended directly within the risen thinking. This would be worthy of the evolved intellect of our age. It would be something quite different from an atavistic clairvoyance. It would mean the opening of dormant faculties of perception present in every man. By meditation and the training of his thinking, he achieved this step. He has described his "Anthroposophy" as "A path of knowledge leading the spiritual in man to the spiritual in the Universe."

Having developed this power of exploring higher worlds and of putting his findings into thoughts, he set out on his investigations into the "Akashic Record." The earth, it appears, is surrounded on a subtle level by an immense field of a spiritual substance known as "akasha" in which is impressed, like a celestrial tape recording, every impulse of human thought, will and emotion. It constitutes therefore a complete record of human and planetary history, and those adepts who have lifted their consciousness until they can "read the akashic record" are able to investigate history at its source without the need of written documents. This Steiner claimed to be able to do, and he was able furthermore to reach right back in his thinking to experience the earlier incarnations of the planet itself. This immense span is covered in his book *Occult Science*.

As a researcher, without preconception, prejudice or dogma, he surveyed back to the dim past of human and planetary evolution, using his developed faculties of cognition. To his astonishment, he came up against the fact of the descent of the Christ as the absolutely central event of evolution, the turning point which gave meaning to history. Be it said that in the 1890's, working in the intellectual and scientific circles in Berlin, he had publicly attacked Christianity. It seems that he must have undergone something comparable to Paul's experience of meeting the Living Christ on the road to Damascus. As Paul must be seen as the first discoverer of the Cosmic Christ, so Steiner rediscovered Him and became His apostle for our century. Of this period in his life he writes in his autobiography: "I stood before the Mystery of Golgotha in a most profound inward festival of knowledge."

From about 1910 on, his entire teaching is Christo-centric. Naturally it does not always conform to church dogma, for this was spiritual research which was able to arrive at esoteric Truth afresh without need to draw on written documents. With a certainty which he claimed to be in line with scientific method, he researched into the unseen worlds, crystallized his findings into thoughts and gave them out in lectures, books and teaching.

What then did he find about the Christ?

His cosmology is always built on his certainty that behind all manifestation in the diversity of the relative world is the great Oneness of Creative Intelligence and Spirit, the Divine Source. "In the beginning was the Word and the Word was with God and the Word was God. By Him were all things made and without Him was not anything made that was made."

Thus the celestrial bodies are not mere gaseous balls but are the spheres of action of exalted spiritual beings. The solar system seen with spiritual knowledge is a huge living organism shot through and through with living thought. Each of the planets represents a vast sphere of forces. Indeed, the movement of the visible planet marks the periphery of this sphere of influence and spiritual quality. We come back again to a recognition of the basic truth of the old concept of the "crystal spheres" of the planets, which was still an active tenet in Shakespeare's day.

The field of action of the highest hierarchy, the Elohim, is the Sun. Since all manifestation in the world of matter is a reflection of spiritual reality on an eternal plane beyond time and space, we must grasp the concept of the spiritual sun. The visible sun is the vortex or channel through which the most exalted beings of light can work. The Lord of these sublime beings is He who was known as the Christos, the Son of God.

The Earth, in this view, is not a dead speck of dust in a vast indifferent mechanism of a cosmos, which some modern astronomers believe it to be. Rather, it is to be seen as a living seed, a planet given the charge of a priceless inheritance—the development of consciousness and the home of a spiritual being who can develop to free will and to God-consciousness. Man, in the spiritual world view, is not a chance accident of evolution in a cosmos wholly indifferent to him. He is part of the primal archetypal vision of the Creator. Though last to appear in physical form, he is, as spiritual archetype, first to be created. Man, in this sense, was there from the very beginning and can become veritably a companion to God, the point where, in thought, God can experience his own reflection.

When I consider the heavens, the moon and the stars which Thou hast ordained, what is man that Thou are mindful of him, or the son of man that Thou visitest him? For Thou hast made him a little lower than the angels and has crowned him with glory and honor.

None can know how many other planets in the Universe carry conscious sentient beings, but planet Earth in our solar system bears a supremely important burden. It was a high compliment that the Sublime Lord of all Light and of the Elohim saw fit to descend and blend His power and life with the stream of earth evolution.

Alice Meynell in her poem, *Christ in the Universe*, writes that ''Our wayside planet bears, as chief treasure, one forsaken grave.''

Steiner's picture of the evolution of the solar system, and the way in which the celestial bodies became related to each other as they are now, is too large a theme to deal with here. His findings do not essentially conflict with the findings of astronomy. Very briefly, be it said that Steiner contends that in early phases, the celestial bodies of the solar system were merged into an enormous whole, shot through with spirit and being. As this condensed, the refined beings of Light found the increasing density intolerable and drew out to a certain distance to play upon the developing earth from outside. Thus appeared what in time became our sun, behind which stood the *spiritual sun*. The result of this withdrawal was that the speed of condensing and hardening greatly increased. Since earth was the field for evolving man, the danger arose that the contracting processes would so harden him that evolution would become impossible. Thus the forces and beings concerned with this condensing also withdrew from the great body to a distance in which their influence could be controlled. Thus appears our moon.

If it be true that all the celestial bodies are spheres of activity of spiritual beings, then we must see that evolution has both a spiritual and a physical aspect. Aeons of time have gone to develop a physical organism capable of carrying a self-conscious "ego." Yet what has been the evolution of that ego itself? If we can take the thought that Man as archetypal idea was created in the beginning, then there must have been a time when this droplet of the Divine Source first began its descent into matter. This is perhaps indicated in Genesis in the verse:

> *And the Lord God formed man of the dust of the ground, and breathed into his nostrils the breath of life and man became a living soul.*

The immortal entity begins to embody itself, though first in a form far different from our present body. This probably takes place far back in the Lemurian epoch, long before Atlantis. By alternating between embodiment and life on the higher planes, the human being gradually gets deeper into the material world, and he is actively involved in working upon the physical vehicle.

Thus we see a spiritual evolution of the entity of man working with the physical evolution.

There comes a time, however, when those beings who were responsible for drawing man down ever deeper into matter had so advanced the hardening and condensing processes on earth that it became likely that human life would become impossible. Had this trend gone on unchecked, then the human being would have become so encased in matter that he would have lost all touch with his spiritual worlds of origin.

Thus, some redemptive deed became necessary.

The Exalted Lord of the Spiritual Sun now took the decision to enter the stream of earth evolution. This great fact is recognized in all the world religions, for it is the supreme turning point in the whole of earth history. The Hindus knew this Being as Vishva Karman. The ancient Persians worshipped Him as Ahura Mazda, Lord of Light, who opposed Ahriman, the Lord of Darkness. The Egyptians knew him as Osiris, and the legend of his dismemberment and rescue by Isis tells of his descent to Earth. The Hebrews awaited His descent as the Messiah. The Buddhists expect Him as the Maitreya. The Mystery Temples of antiquity foresaw the redemptive descent of the God of Light who would reverse the trend of hardening into matter. Precisely how and when the Christos would enter earth, they could not know, but the initiates knew that when the event happened they would be aware of it, since the whole aura of the earth would change and be shot through with light. The descent of the Christ Being is a unique event in history in which a God for the first and only time experiences human death. There had, of course, been many cases of divine beings temporarily taking over the individuality of a man. This is often described in Greek legend but is quite different from the actual identification with man so as to suffer and experience death.

Steiner describes the event which can be seen by all initiates in whom the inner faculties of vision are developed. To enter earth evolution, the Christos needed a perfected human instrument. This was Jesus. The Holy Spirit had prepared this vehicle through long periods. That a human body could carry in himself the Cosmic Being who had declared himself as "I AM THAT I AM," implies the highest possible preparation. In Jesus there flow together two streams, the one bringing all the Wisdom of the Ages, the other pure love and compassion. The Gospel of Matthew indicates the royal lineage from Solomon and David to whom the three Wise Men are drawn. They represent a Wisdom tradition going back to the original Zoroaster. The Gospel of Luke describes the soul of Innocence who draws to himself the simple shepherds and the creatures of nature. How these two merge is an occult mystery which Steiner investigated. It explains the remarkable discrepancies between the two Gospel stories. Suffice it to say that we are being told of the preparation of the sublime vehicle who could receive the Cosmic Christ.

The moment of entry is seen to be the Baptism by John in Jordan. Then the individuality of Jesus gave place to the Christ Being, the Cosmic I AM. At the moment when "the Holy Ghost descended in the form of a dove," this Exalted Being took over the human body. For the next three years, it is the Christ who is speaking in Jesus. The previous thirty years had been a preparation of the vehicle.

This view of the event, drawn from esoteric vision, of course differs from the tacit assumption that the Christ was born in Jesus as a babe. We are invited to rethink. There is usually such close association of Jesus with the Christ that the concept of the descent of the God of Light is lost. Esoteric Christianity sees Jesus as the human vehicle for the Cosmic Being of the Christ. This was clearly accepted in the first two centuries by the followers of Christ. They celebrated the "Christ-Mass," the true birth of the Christ, on January 6, Epiphany, the day of the Baptism. It was only in the fourth century A.D. that Christmas was moved forward to the date of the birth of the babe on December 25. This suggests that the occult knowledge of the descent of the God of Light was too difficult to be generally understood when all Roman citizens were baptized into the Christian faith. Therefore, the knowledge was lost and indeed was driven underground as heresy.

It is, however, most significant that the Gospels of Mark and John both begin with the Baptism in Jordan and only deal with the three last years. Matthew and Luke tell the story of the birth of Jesus, in both cases in what is really a surprisingly short introduction, and then quickly move on to the Baptism. The early followers of Christ were chiefly interested in celebrating the Baptism and the Resurrection rather than the birth and the Crucifixion, for they still knew of this sublime Event of the descent of the Christ.

The events during the three years of His life in Jesus are to be seen as the continuous process of incarnation of the Cosmic I AM. Thus, the temptation marks the takeover of the astral body of Jesus, the Transfiguration of the complete mastery of the etheric body. When on the Cross He called out the words, "It is finished," it amounted to a triumphant declaration that matter had been fully mastered, the complete incarnation was achieved and death conquered.

This Deed of Christ is to be seen as the absolute turning point in history and evolution. It may be said to have reversed the Fall of Man. It indeed starts the Ascent of Man, opening the possibility of his recovering his lost knowledge of the Spiritual Worlds.

Steiner spoke always of the "Mystery of Golgotha," thus implying that Christ achieved thereby a transformation of the ancient mysteries which in the temples of antiquity initiated pupils into esoteric knowledge of the higher worlds. So profound is the Mystery of Golgotha that we only begin to understand its implications for the future of mankind. At that moment, the Christ Impulse entered into earthly evolution and continues to work as a leaven to redeem the human soul and body.

A God experienced human death. At the moment when the

blood ran into the earth from the body on the Cross, the whole aura of the earth was changed. Steiner, in a lecture called ''The Etherization of the Blood'' describes how the divine blood was transmuted onto an etheric level so that it was able to extend into the whole ''ether body'' of the earth. It was ''potentized'' in the sense that the word is used in homoeopathy. While the body of Jesus lay dead, the Christ being became the helper and redeemer of the souls of the dead who had lost their divine nature. The Greek conviction was that the dead were as shades. Achilles, when Odysseus visited him in Hades, said that it was ''better to be a beggar on earth than a king in the realm of the shades.'' The entry of the Christ into what we now call the Borderland brought a flooding of light and hope. Much the same situation holds good today. So many souls who ''go over'' with no understanding or belief in the immortality of the soul find themselves as ''shades'' in a surrounding of gloom and obscurity and may even not know that they are dead. The Living Christ in this age comes again to redeem lost souls.

Christ's resurrection overcame death. A spiritual being has to ''embody'' itself in whatever sheath is necessary for it to enter another plane of being. Thus a physical body with a hard skeleton is essential if it wishes to incarnate on earth. If it enters a gaseous or a liquid planet, then a gaseous, fiery or viscous body will be needed. When its task is finished, the particles of the sheath should be dispersed and should return to their source.

Thus, the survival of the corpse is seen as something essentially unnatural. ''By man came death.'' As the etheric forces return after death to the great etheric pool, so it was meant that the physical particles should dissolve without leaving the corpse. The Christ had such power that He could control even the physical body, so that the corpse disappeared. Instead of the etheric body dispersing, He was then able to hold it together in a human form which appeared identical with the physical. By so doing, He demonstrated that man will in time be able to overcome death and dematerialize the physical sheath when it has done its task.

The descent of the Christ meant the entry of an Impulse into the dying body of the earth. It checked the tendency to overhardening and condensing which was present in evolution through the working of the adversary forces. Hence, from that Easter Sunday the possibility of rising again was given to man.

Redemption from the ultimate hardening into matter is thereby achieved. Had the Christ not descended, souls upon earth would have become so deeply embedded in matter that all knowledge of the spiritual worlds would have been lost.

For six weeks, the Risen Christ moved among the disciples in the Resurrection Body, able to come and go and be in more than one place at a time. Thus, John in his last sentence in his Gospel writes that if all the deeds of Christ were to be written down, "I suppose that even the world itself could not contain the books that should be written."

Then came the Ascension, when the disciples appeared to lose Him as He was taken "up to heaven." Here, Steiner gives an illuminating interpretation. The Christ has taken over the direction of the life of the earth. Thus he moves into the "higher" realm of the *etheric* which, being the life structure which permeates all form and holds together the particles of substance, is absolutely ubiquitous. He disappears to physical view, but from now on is everywhere and within the etheric body of every plant, tree, animal or man. "I am with you always, even to the end of the earth cycle." Certain medieval maps of the globe show the Christ standing behind the earth and holding it, so that head, hands and feet just appear. The following poem by Joseph Plunkett attempts to express the stupendous truth.

> *I see his blood upon the rose*
> *And in the stars the glory of his eyes,*
> *His body gleams amid eternal snows,*
> *His tears fall from the skies.*

I see his face in every flower;
The thunder and the singing of the birds
Are but his voice—and carven by his power
Rocks are his written words.

All pathways by his feet are worn,
His strong heart stirs the ever-beating sea,
His crown of thorns is twined with every thorn,
His cross is every tree.

The Ascension is to be seen as a deed for all men. As the physical sun shines on all, so every human being is redeemed by the Deed of Christ and by His sacrifice in taking over the Regency of the etheric earth. The event of Pentecost at Whitsuntide offered the possibility that the individual soul, who from within itself made the approach, could be flooded with Christ Power. Here the Comforter, the Holy Spirit, came in the form of the Gifts of the Spirit on the first Pentecost. Thus, Whitsun is a festival for the redemption of the individual ego in its attempt to overcome the desires of the lower self and surrender to the Higher Self. Each man has his Higher Self or spiritual principle, and this is Christ-filled.

The two festivals, Ascension and Pentecost, come alive for our time in a wonderful way. The Christ Impulse floods all life, rejuvenating the soul. No longer need man harden into matter and lose touch with the higher worlds. The Ascent of Man has begun as a result of the Christ Deed. The redemption of the race has been begun: To quote the last words of Christopher Smart's "Song to David":

> *And now the matchless deed's achieved,*
> *Determined, dared and done.*

It needs, however, the inner initiative of the individual soul to lift and open itself to the entry of the Christ. This is the task of our age. To quote Steiner: ''The supreme mystery of the age in which we are living is the Second Coming of Christ—that is its true nature.''

Now we see the meaning of the Second Coming. The Christ is now overlighting all mankind. He is present everywhere in the etheric. If men can lift their consciousness into this supersensible, invisible realm, they will find Him. In this sense, the Second Coming has already happened. It is for us to bring it to individual consciousness and realization.

Our epoch is the Cosmic Whitsuntide when the individual ego can, through its own conscious initiative, unite with the I AM. This is Teilhard's ''homing upon the Omega point.'' This fulfills the age and leads us through into the new epoch.

We see that the ''Body of Christ'' is being formed everywhere by the individual souls who unite themselves with Him. Each is like a blood corpuscle in this Body and is essentially the New Age Society, bound by the Love for the Divine in all things and in each other.

There is clearly no need for the Christ to incarnate again and live through a physical body and so pass through death. That was done once and need not be repeated. He can appear in a thousand places at the same time anywhere in the world. In the resurrection body, he can appear and then mysteriously withdraw, and there are more and more cases of this happening since the middle of our century. Nor need He always appear in the traditional white robe. As Lord and Creator of all Life, he can overlight any human form. He has, with the eye of vision, been seen as the great scholar in academic robes, for surely He is the master scientist, the Lord of all Wisdom. He could appear in the Olympic Games to show what sublime beauty and achievement is possible with the human body. He could overlight a politician or public figure, speaking through him in the Risen Language of the spirit. As a new society is formed out of the chaos of our age, this Redeeming Power of the Second Coming may be expected in infinitely varied fields.

Steiner himself must have experienced something of Paul's vision at the Gates of Damascus. He tells us that more and more people from now onwards and through into the coming centuries will have the same experience and know with absolute certainty that the Living Christ exists.

Thus, the wonder of our age is that through all the darkness and negation, the Christ Impulse is flooding. There is a resurgence of light and a new consciousness which can redeem the pollution of the planet through the instrument of the individual souls who receive the Power of the Spirit and allow it to pour through them for the healing of mankind. Christ is the Great Healer who can restore the imbalanced body to its true relation to the Whole. To quote from the Creed of the Christian Community, the Church founded by Steiner: ''He will in time unite for the advancement of the world with those whom through their bearing He can wrest from the death of matter.''

By its nature, esoteric Christianity contains concepts so advanced that they could not possibly have been accepted by the general public in the earth Church or even in our time. Truth, however, is so many-faceted that there need be no essential conflict. If we are drawn to accept that the Christ is a Cosmic Being who entered into the human vehicle of Jesus, this does not in any way reduce the stature of Jesus. Rather does it raise and expand the whole picture of Christianity as the impulse which can lead to a true world religion. Christ is not merely a great teacher. Christianity, in Steiner's phrase, is a mystical fact, the greatest event in history. The entry of the Cosmic Christ for all men relates Christianity to the other great religions.

The recognition of Jesus as the vehicle of the Christ places Him in His true relation to the other prophets. The Buddha prepared the way 600 years before the Event of Golgotha by showing the path to enlightenment. Six hundred years after it, Mohammed made his revelations of the One God. Modern research, particuarly into the works of the Islamic sage, Ibn al'Arabi, reveals that the esoteric core of Islam is truly teaching knowledge of the Cosmic Christ. As we recognize the reality of the spiritual worlds, we shall learn that the Buddha is now working in close association with Christ for the redemption of mankind through illumination of understanding. The Master Jesus is ever present with us as leader of the group of the great spiritual Masters. Thus, this concept of the Cosmic Christ helps us to lift clear of the apparent contradictions between the religions and points the way to a vision which unites all men who have found their way to the health-giving power of the Christ Impulse. What name we give does not matter. We are united in recognition and worship of the Lord of Light.

4 | Thoughts on the Second Coming

WHAT REALLY IS HAPPENING to us now?

Profound changes are afoot on the inner and outer planes. Where may we be by this time next year? Our most real problem is how to learn to move creatively into and through change. The note of an Apocalyptic age is: "Behold I make all things new." If this is fulfilled, then what will guide us through the changing world with courage in situations which may have no precedent?

The Apocalyptic passages in Matthew 24, Luke 17 and the Book of Revelation speak to our age. It may literally have become true that "this generation shall not pass away but these words will be fulfilled." Mankind has now reached that evolutionary point when the breakthrough beyond egoism becomes possible and the soul sets forth on the quest for its real home. Teilhard de Chardin called the process "homing upon the Omega Point" and knew that this ultimate Being was the Divine Individuality who said "I am Alpha and Omega, the First and the Last."

In the Book of Revelation, it is described how the Beast, having made war in Heaven against Michael and his angels, is driven down to earth, "having great wrath because he knoweth that he hath but a short time." Earth enters into great tribulation with "wars and rumors of wars . . . famines and pestilences and earthquakes in divers places," but "after the tribulation they shall see the Son of Man coming in the clouds of heaven with power and great glory" and the "trumpeting of the angels." Then comes the Fall of Babylon, City of Abominations, symbol for all that human avarice, lust and egoism has brought about. And after that the descent of New Jerusalem "like a bride adorned for her husband." Redeemed Man is united with the higher and Christ-filled Self and enters a new golden age when the beast is chained a thousand years in the abyss.

This great piece of visionary allegory appears to refer to the passage from the Piscean to the Aquarian Age. We are all summoned to take part in this event. The young who now reach the height of strength and responsibility will carry the great changes, and many have surely incarnated for this deliberate purpose. Those who are of advancing years will soon be released from bodily limitation, but since for soul and spirit there is no death, they will still be very much involved from the other side, working for the Coming of the Light and the redemption of the earth and man.

"Who is this King of Glory?" He is that exalted Being who said to Moses, "I AM THAT I AM." The great religions knew of His coming. We are grasping the tremendous conception of the Cosmic Christ. The descent of the Eternal I AM into the body of the living Earth is obviously such an advanced esoteric vision that it could not have been taught as Church doctrine when it was decreed that the whole Roman Empire should become Christian. A simpler story was needed to give the great truth to all folk. So there came about a division into the two streams of exoteric and esoteric Christianity, complementary to each other. On the one hand, there was the orthodox Church doctrine which all could understand, and on the other, the esoteric knowledge and teaching, running like a secret underground stream, often suppressed as heresy, but reappearing in each age in a form suitable for the time. It is this hidden wisdom that re-emerges to illumine our age and gives the clue to the nature of the Second Coming. As the physical sun lights and warms all men and contains all life, so the Spiritual Sun, the I AM, overlights all mankind of every race and creed. The great religions all present facets of the Divine Truth.

May it be that we approach a true World Religion, uniting all in the worship of the God of Universal Light?

Now expectation intensifies and the invocation goes up for Christ to return to earth. Of course, in one sense He has never left, for He is everywhere, working as an impulse of Love and life within the etheric field, the vital forces of earth, and therefore within every form. Thus the Cosmic Christ, Lord of the Solar Logos, is also the energy within the cell and nuclear center, and yet, at the same time, He is the personal Savior who knocks at the door of the heart.

We must indeed stretch our minds to grasp the scale of the picture.

Most of those who can attune innerly to higher levels of intelligence indicate that profoundly significant events are imminent. We are on the brink of a very important step forward, apocalyptic, perhaps, in its nature, but a prelude to the Great Coming of the Being of Light, the I AM, Limitless Love and Truth, the Christos.

This exalted Being is the very Life of the great Oneness. He is present within the heart that is ready to receive Him, for this is the most immediate way of His Coming. The little "I am" can unite with the Great I AM. Think of the I AM sayings, such as:

"I am with you always, even to the end of the world epoch."
"I am the Light of the World."
"I am the Resurrection and the Life."

(Note that He did not say *I am resurrected and alive* but *I am the Life*.)

The whole tradition and technique of Contemplative Prayer is built upon such phrases, spoken silently within the mind until it seems that He Himself is speaking them, giving the experience that He is in the very center of consciousness.

Let us now consider that amazing document, the Gospel of St. Thomas. This consists of some 120 aphorisms or "Logia" spoken by Christ Jesus on the Oneness theme, and it seems to bear out our understanding of the spiritual world view. Thomas appears to have been the one among the Apostles who really grasped that his Lord *was* the Living Oneness, the Living One, who could not possibly die. His apparent death puzzled him more than His resurrection. In Logia 13, Thomas tells a delightful story.

"Jesus says to him: 'I am not thy Master, because thou hast drunk, thou hast become drunk from the bubbling spring which I have measured out.' And He took him aside and said three words to him. Now when Thomas came to his companions they asked him, 'What did Jesus say to you?' Thomas said to them: 'If I tell you one of the words he said to me, you would take up stones and throw them at me, and fire will come from the stones and burn you up.' " [We are not told what the words were, but they must in effect have been 'I am you', 'We are One.']

Here are a few examples of the Oneness Thinking numbered for reference as in the Gospel:

Logia

113 *"The Kingdom is spread on earth and men do not see it."*

 77 *"I am the light that is above them all. I am the All and the All came forth from me and the All attained to me. Cleave the wood; I am there. Lift the stone and you will find me there."*

 59 *"Search for the living One as long as you live, lest you die and are unable to do so."*

 52 *"You have dismissed the Living One and speak about the dead."*

108 *"Whoever drinks my words from me shall become as I am and I myself will become he and that which is hidden shall be revealed."*

106 *"When you make the two one, you shall become sons of men."* (i.e. when you in your consciousness overcome the separation.)

51 *"What you expect has come but you know it not."*

67 *"Whoever knows the Universe but fails to know himself lacks everything."*

50 *"If they say to you From where have you originated, say We have come from the Light, where Light originated through itself and reveals itself in our image."*

19 *"Whoever finds the explanation of these words will not taste death."*

111 *"The heavens and the earth will be rolled out in your presence but he who lives on the Living One shall see neither death nor fear."*

10 *"I have cast fire on the world and see, I guard it until the world is afire."*

Here surely is the Gnosis, the Vision of Wholeness. The last aphorisms suggest the apocaltyptic cleansing, but, where the Living One is within the aura and heart, there is nothing to fear. And the phrase "Living One" and "Living Oneness" are clearly interchangeable. It is not surprising that Thomas found his way to India to carry his Gospel to the culture that really had the Vision of Wholeness.

What then may we expect in the time that has now come upon us? Our primary concern must surely be with the awakening of the Living One within the Heart. This could be like a flood of living energy. We are assured by Alice Bailey in her "Tibetan" teachings that the flow of energies has been stepped up since 1975 to prepare the way for greater events. This mounting flood of the waters of Aquarius will undermine and wash away what is negative. It is like a rising tide. These energies, imbued with Light and Life and Love, are directed to bringing a harmony of all life. They will be furiously resisted by the adversary forces. The present manifestations of violence, cruelty and disorder are the workings of the Beast. But every dying process is, we know, a prelude to renewal, and there can be no real renewal without a dying of the old. We are watching the beginning of a process that will sweep away that which is geared to the old laws of separation. The New is to be based on cooperation and giving, and service of the Divine Will and the Whole.

The Apocalyptic picture undoubtedly implies a separation into two levels. Those souls attuned sufficiently to receive the Christ power will be lifted into His Body and experience a flooding of heart and mind with a love overflowing to all other beings. What a theme for science fiction! Those who are not ready are not lost souls but will be shepherded by Him on some lower planetary level to be given their opportunity at a later round. Thus, as the pressure of events reaches its climax, there seems bound to be some such separation. There may well be a building up of tension to breaking point, and then in despair and desperation, mankind will call upon God and Christ. Then, as is borne out in history by the doctrine of the Avatars, the Savior will appear. His power is backed by all the forces of the Light, and His Coming will be supported by the White Brotherhood of the Angelic World and by all those human beings now sojourning on the eternal plane who have found the Christ—a goodly army indeed.

Already, we are told, many have accepted the Christ impulse and teachings into their auras, though not yet into their thinking or active lives; but when the moment comes the seed left in the aura will grow and yield enormously. This implies that the changes need not be as drastic as some have feared. The new consciousness could come as a revelation, "in the twinkling of an eye." There could be a collapse and disintegration of negative thought forms. The very drive and initiative now manifesting so powerfully in violence and cruelty could give way before the unlimited energies of the Light.

It must be quite clear that Christ, having once incarnated and gone through human death, does not need to repeat that Deed. This does not preclude his appearing again in the resurrection body in all semblance like a man. Already there are many strange stories in moments of desperate suffering, of the appearance of one who by his presence is able to transform the situation. There are communications received by those telepathically attuned that indicate a personal reappearance of the Christ in the near future. Many are convinced He will reveal Himself and be seen, even on television, and known by the quality of His being and teaching. In preparation for these events, it appears that the Masters, that group of human beings known as the Hierarchy, so advanced that for some centuries they have worked to help mankind from the invisible planes, are actually now taking on embodiment so as to prepare the way for the reappearance of the Christ.

Of course, we have had the warning to beware of false Christs and those who say "Lo, here is Christ, or there." There is no need to take any sort of dogmatic attitude, since this immense event is very complex. There seems to be no reason why the Lord of the Solar Logos, present throughout the etheric field of Earth, could not also, as an aspect of His supernal Being, decide to manifest in a resurrection body, appearing in many places at the same time or, if he willed, in one. We are not called on either to believe or disbelieve that He will personally appear in a visible body. If it happens, we shall know it, so there is no need to argue! If He is to remain invisible but act as a living impulse awakening the heart with a surge and overspill of joy and love for all life, then we shall know and experience that—and rejoice. Jubilate! In some sense, of course, He has always been here. If He is indeed present invisibly throughout the whole etheric field of the earth, then He is truly within the etheric body of every form, every tree and flower, every crystal and animal. But with our normal intellectual processes, we cannot consciously experience this. If we can raise our thinking and awareness into the etheric field, there we shall find Him. We should then, as far as we are individually concerned, experience an aspect of the Second Coming by lifting a pre-existent condition into consciousness.

Clearly, we must stretch our thinking wide. It is a cosmic picture, not a dogmatic and sectarian belief. We speak of the Cosmic

Christ, the Universal Being of All Light, who called Himself "Limitless Love and Truth." We must grasp the concept of the Christ Impulse working like a leaven within all life and yet in personal relationship to every human being.

The great event may happen in many different ways. What matters is that we awaken to the scale of current events and the urgency of present developments. That the Coming, whatever form it may take, is imminent, is agreed by all the different teachers and seers who are attuned to the higher planes. "Look up for thy redemption draweth nigh." It is for us to awaken. The transformation of man is taking place and is palpably accelerating. If we can but attune innerly, dedicate ourselves to service of the Divine Will and open the heart to the Christ Impulse, then there is no cause for worry. The only real source of anxiety would be that we slept through these events and failed to see what is afoot. So, like the Wise Virgins, let us keep our lamps trimmed. Individual human initiative and invocation is clearly the essential factor, since, as said before, these spiritual impulses will not violate our free will. The inner dedication achieved, we may then move forward boldly into the unknown, certain that we are being guided through apocalyptic days and that beyond tribulation, a new society is coming to birth.

We are co-creators of that which truly is the Body of Christ. This is the New Jerusalem. And the change of consciousness could come "in the twinkling of an eye."

The Christ Event will obviously concern all mankind. It must have the effect of lifting us above sectarian division. It demonstrates the truth that, despite internal divisions, mankind is one great family.

This picture brings an immense hope. The Higher worlds of spirit know that a cleansing of Earth must be achieved. If men fail to respond and adjust, they must suffer. But we are assured that the Angels of Destiny are concerned to reduce suffering as much as possible in the necessary changes—which will inevitably come and could come rapidly. There is ultimately no need for fear. We could go smoothly into another world condition, for the changes have already taken place on the subtle and invisible levels, and only as an end process do they become manifest on the physical. As we have already said, the Christ Light has been allowed to impregnate the human aura, even if as yet it does not show outwardly in conscious understanding. Thus, when the time comes, very many people may find they are ready to accept and acknowledge the living Christ. His reappearance would bring such a surge of creative love and joy that it could veritably inaugurate the true brotherhood of man.

Here are the closing words of the Revelation of St. John the Divine.

> *I Jesus have sent mine angel to testify unto you these things. I am the root and the offspring of David and the bright and morning star.*
>
> *And the Spirit and the bride say, Come. And let him that heareth say, Come. And let him that is athirst come. And whosoever will, let him take the water of life freely.*
>
> *He which testifieth these things saith, Surely I come quickly. Amen. Even so, come, Lord Jesus.*

SOME QUOTATIONS ABOUT THE SECOND COMING

Quotations from Lectures by Rudolf Steiner:

> *The supreme mystery of the age in which we are living is the second Coming of Christ—that is its true nature. (1910)*

> *We are now able to grasp quite a different aspect of Spiritual Science. We realize that it is a preparation for the actual event of the new appearance of Christ. Christ will appear again in so far as with their etheric sight men will raise themselves to Him. Spiritual Science is offered as a means of preparing men to recognize the*

return of Christ, in order that it shall not be their misfortune to overlook this event but that they shall be mature enough to grasp the great happening of the Second Coming. Men will be capable of seeing etheric bodies—and among them also the etheric body of Christ—i.e. they will grow into a world where Christ will be revealed to their newly awakened faculties. It will then be no longer necessary to amass all kinds of documentary evidence to prove the existence of Christ. There will be eye-witnesses of the presence of the Living Christ, men who will know Him in His etheric body. And from this experience they will realize that this is the same Being who at the beginning of our era fulfilled the Mystery of Golgotha— that He is indeed the Christ. Just as Paul at Damascus was convinced at that time:—"This is the Christ" — so there will be men whose experiences in the etheric world will convince them that in very truth Christ lives." (1910)

All that can be gained by a mastery of material forces is insignificant compared with what will be given to men who have experienced in their souls the awakening through Christ, Who is now entering human evolution . . . People will be able to recognize and to comprehend that which has its beginning in the Twentieth Century—the Etheric Christ in place of the Physical Christ of Palestine. We have reached that point of time when the Etheric Christ enters the light of the earth. (1911)

From Teilhard de Chardin, *"Le Milieu Divin"* (Epilogue):

Christ will only come soon if we ardently expect Him. It is an accumulation of desires that should cause the Pleroma to burst upon us. We Christians have been charged with keeping the flame of desire ever alive in the world. No doubt our prayers and actions are conscientiously directed to bringing about "The coming of God's Kingdom." But in fact how many of us are genuinely moved in the depths of our hearts by the wild hope that our earth will be recast? Who is there who sets a course in the midst of our darkness towards the first glimmer of a real dawn? At all costs we must renew in ourselves the desire and the hope for the great Coming . . . Let us look at the earth around us. What is happening under our eyes within the mass of peoples? What is the cause of this disorder in society, this uneasy agitation, these swelling waves, these whirling and mingling currents and these turbulent and formidable new impulses? Mankind is visibly passing through a crisis of growth. Mankind is becoming dimly aware of its shortcomings and its capacities. And it sees the universe growing luminous like the horizon just before sunrise. It has a sense of premonition and of expectation . . . The world can no more have two summits than a circumference can have two centers. The star for which the world is waiting, without yet being able to give it a name, or rightly appreciate its true transcendence, or even recognize the most spiritual and divine of its rays, is, necessarily, Christ Himself, in whom we hope. To desire the Parousia, all we have to do is to let the very heart of the earth, as we Christianize it, beat within us.

From The Bhagavad Gita:

Whenever there is a withering of the law and an uprising of lawlessness on all sides, then I manifest Myself.

For the salvation of the righteous and the destruction of such as do evil, for the firm establishing of the Law, I come to birth age after age.

From The Reappearance of the Christ by Alice Bailey, Chapter 1:

Right down the ages, in many world cycles and in many countries (and today in all) great points of tension have occurred which have been characterized by a hopeful sense of expectancy. Some one is expected and His coming is anticipated . . . The coming of the Avatar, the advent of a Coming One and, in terms of today, the reappearance of the Christ, are the keynotes of the prevalent expectancy. When the times are ripe, the invocation of the masses is strident enough and the faith of those who know is keen enough, then always He has come and today will be no exception to this ancient rule or to this universal law. For decades, the reappearance of the Christ, the Avatar, has been anticipated by the faithful in both hemispheres—not only by the Christian faithful, but by those who look for Maitreya and for the Bodhisattva as well as those who expect the Imam Mahdi . . .

The Avatars themselves can become events in the life of our planet; toward Them every eye can look and all men can be affected . . . They frequently create crises in order to bring to an end the old and the undesirable and make way for new and more suitable forms for the evolving life of God Immanent in Nature. They come when evil is rampant. For this reason, if for no other, an Avatar may be looked for today. The necessary stage is set for the reappearance of the Christ.

5 | Michael and All Angels

ANGELS—what a part these radiant creatures played in the consciousness of the Age of Faith! What a theme they have been for art and architecture, and with what certainty our forebears represented them as a great reality. Think of the fabulous timber roofs in Suffolk and Somerset churches thronged with angels with wings outspread around the roof bosses and on the hammer beams, and the exquisite Angel Choir at Lincoln with beautiful winged beings in the spandrels of all the arches. Think of Fra Angelico's Angel of the Annunciation. Go to a gallery of medieval and renaissance paintings, or even turn over a volume of illustration, with the express purpose of studying angels. The Kingdom of Angels was clearly accepted as an absolute certainty and a factor of supreme importance in life, for these glorious beings were the intermediaries between Heaven and Earth.

Then inevitably, with the coming of our rational and intellectual age, doubt crept in. How could they exist if we can't see them or prove them to our physical senses? And how could they operate such great wings without the breast bone of a bird? The modern mind has lost touch and achieved disbelief. We intone such high sounding phrases as "Therefore with Angels and Archangels and with all the company of heaven, we laud and magnify thy glorious Name, evermore praising thee and saying: Holy, holy, holy, Lord God of Hosts, heaven and earth are full of thy glory . . ." But do we really believe them or treat them only as a manner of speaking and a survival of superstition? Or may the angels still be real?

Now, the holistic world view implies the subdividing of thought into myriads of beings of whom the complexity of the material world is a reflection. Spiritual research and vision rediscovers the angelic kingdoms. We have lost the angels simply because we have reduced our seeing to "single vision." It would indeed be gross superstition to think we could see angels with our physical eyes. It needs subtler senses to observe the beings within form on a more rarified vibration.

To those who have clairvoyant vision, the angels appear as figures of pure light from which great auras of radiant colored light ray out, giving the effect of wings. Feathered wings as a symbol are valid enough, since these beings exist within the realm of levity, as free of gravity as is a flame, or soaring to the heights and hovering like a bird.

Geoffrey Hodson was one of those who could see the angels, and his fine book *The Kingdom of the Gods* describes the angelic hierarchies and his direct experience of them. It is illustrated by an artist to whom he described the great Devas of the mountains, forests, seas and rivers. Among the myriad throng of celestial beings, these are the guardians and architects of nature's forms.

I have a friend with highly developed psychic powers who one day was directed by her Higher Guide to photograph a certain tree. This she obediently did, seeing nothing especially noteworthy about the subject. When the film was developed, there appeared a great structure of colored light in front of the tree, a central figure or column of light ten feet tall, from which radiated glorious tippling beams of gold and pink and magenta and pale violet, some forty feet high. There is no possibility that this could have been either a fake or a faulty film. And it is beautiful. How rich a world exists just beyond the borders of normal vision, truly a world of "faery."

> *The angels keep their ancient places*
> *Turn by a stone and start a wing.*

> *'Tis ye, 'tis your estranged faces*
> *That miss the many-splendored thing.*
>
> *(Francis Thompson)*

We have spoken of the Oceans of Being which penetrate ethereal space. It is a noble conception that the Almighty Mind, moving from the Absolute into Creation, must have allowed itself to manifest in great spheres of consciousness and quality, a differentiation of the Whole into facets of force and energy. These oceans of energy are seen to be alive, sentient and operative, not mere mechanical energy but forces of wisdom, will and thought. Moses, realizing that Divine Law worked through such seas or reservoirs of living being, first promulgated a science of the Angels. In all the Essene teachings, which were founded on the Mosaic vision, the spheres of the angels were held to be energies which were self-actuating and all working in harmony with the Law for the advancement of life and consciousness. The human being is at every point and moment in touch with these energies.

St. Augustine wrote, concerning creation:

> *Things were rather in the Angelic Mind than in Nature - that is to say that the Angels perceived and knew all things in their thoughts before they could spring into actual existence. God never works but through them.*

Then, in Christian doctrine appeared the teachings on the Nine Heavenly Hierarchies:

The Cherubim, the Seraphim, the Thrones,

The Principalities, Powers and Mights,

The Archai, the Archangels and the Angels.

Dionysus the Areopagite used the resounding Greek names for the second triplicate: Kyriotetes: Exusiai: Dynamis.

These are all part of the Consciousness of God and are overlighted by the Elohim of whom Christ is the Lord.

In his researches into the spiritual worlds and the evolution of our planet, Steiner finds the same ninefold grouping of angelic beings and uses the more modern nomenclature:

Spirits of Will, Spirits of Motion, Spirits of Love,
Spirits of Wisdom, Motion, Personality,
Time Spirits, Spirits of Fire, Angels or Spirits of
Twilight.

The Archai or Time Spirits are the exalted beings who overlight the epochs of evolving civilization. The Archangels are seen as the rulers of the historical periods. They are closely related to the Folk-Souls of the nations and are concerned with the unfolding destiny of man. Thus, it is recognized that the great Archangel Michael (pronounced Michaël) was in charge in the centuries leading up to the descent of Christ, that Gabriel was the archangel of our Western civilization as it grew, but that Michael again took over the regency of the heavenly force on Earth at the end of the nineteenth century. Steiner was able to pinpoint the date as 1879, so we have just passed a significant centenary. We are now in another "Michael Age" and must recognize him as the Archangel who is watching over the birth of the New Age.

Who then is Michael? What does the Michael Impulse mean?

The archangel is variously called "Prince of Heaven", "Countenance of the Christ", "Wielder of the Sword of Light", "Regent of the Heavenly Forces upon Earth", "Lord of the Cosmic Intelligence."

It is helpful to think of the "Michael Impulse", in the same way as we speak of the "Christ Impulse." We are trying to grasp the immense and significant phenomenon of our time—that energies or forces appear to be flooding into human consciousness from the higher planes of the universe to cleanse our planet and transform mankind. If this be true, it would clearly be a factor of supreme importance in solving the great planetary problems that human greed and ignorance have produced. Once we grasp the holistic world picture, we recognize that there are many levels or grades of consciousness and vibration, our physical gravity world being the lowest and densest. As Dante explored up the nine terraces to the Empyrean, so can we envisage tier upon tier of ever subtler and more refined vibration. All these planes or realms interpenetrate, since each operates on a different frequency and so is invisible to those below it. The subtler planes traverse and interpenetrate the denser. So we may recover the concept of the angelic hierarchies as referring to a phenomenon of reality and importance in our lives.

The angels, the lowest of the nine heavenly hierarchies, are nearest to man. It appears that their task is to help and guide the human being while sojourning on the earth plane. Now, the angelic worlds are all part of the Thought of God. They cannot be separated from it. Their delight is to serve the Will of God as it operates harmoniously through the Divine Law. The angels are not, therefore, concerned with free will as such. That is the peculiar gift to mankind. How much trouble it has caused and what infinite and glorious possibilities it implies!

"When I consider the heavens, the work of Thy hands which Thou hast ordained, what is man that thou art mindful of him and the Son of Man that thou visitest him, for Thou hast made him a little lower than the angels, and crowned him with glory and honour."

Humanity has been called the Tenth Hierarchy, a great continuum of souls in evolution towards moral freedom and creativity. To us has been given this gift of free will, and to learn to use it to the glory of God in free creativity, we have to pass through a very difficult and arduous phase of development. The Fall involves separation (apparently) from the Will of God. Human consciousness has had to go through the centuries of separation, each human being feeling himself to be an isolated ego among a myriad of separate things and objects and people. All sense of the oneness of life is inevitably lost, and the spiritual worlds, to intellectual vision, simply fade away. Now we are in process of awakening the dormant faculties which can begin again to know these worlds and rediscover the reality of the angels.

Only a proportion of souls from this human hierarchy are in incarnation at any one moment—4,000,000,000, in our time. The rest are sojourning in higher planes, and many are very closely related to earth life, helping us through this difficult and dramatic age. We each have a Higher Self, that parental being who is the spiritual aspect of our human nature. The Higher Self can truly be the channel for our meditation and prayer to the angelic worlds and to the unknowable God. We also, it appears, each have our Angel, who is responsible for the guiding of our destiny. We may also have a Guide who is human, not angelic. He will be one we knew and loved in an earlier life and is perhaps an advanced soul who does not need to incarnate again.

If we can take the spiritual world view and live as if it were true, then we may begin really to cooperate with our Higher Self, our angel and our guide. They, poor dears, have gone on so long guiding and loving us without any recognition or thanks on our part! Now what joy if we once wake up to their existence and their nearness and call for their cooperation. Always remember that, since man is learning freedom, the angelic worlds may not interfere or take over unless invited and invoked. Ours is the initiative in calling on their help. But when we *do* call, their response is immediate.

All the time, they are staging situations which are designed to test us and develop our character. They lead us up to the point of choice and then stand back to watch what we will do. How often we fall back into old reactions and habit patterns! What possibilities of new creative action open up if we could truly live in the moment in conscious touch with our angels! This is a factor of first importance as we live through the changes which herald the New Age.

In quite practical ways, they can work with us. They wait on our invitation, and we should be prepared to use them. For instance, we should never drive out in a car without calling on our angel for protection. Dark attack is possible at any unexpected moment, for the adversary forces are always seeking opportunities to impede the soul reaching for the light. So accidents may be avoided through our angelic protection. Speak innerly to your angel. Act as if you believed in them and their love, and an inner certainty will grow as to the reality of their presence.

But not only are they useful to us. We are also important to the angelic world. Our Spiritual Teachers tell us that *prayer is the most important deterrent against the forces of evil in the world today.* One person working within the Light is able to offset a thousand working against it. Each one of us is asked daily to send our Light to the Spiritual Hierarchy. Due to the escalating world situation, the Angelic World needs more of our Light Energy to help alleviate the mounting stress and assist in the affairs of men. Our prayer, whether directed or in general, is the essential ingredient for their working on the earth plane. Whenever we have a few spare moments, as well as at our time of meditation, we can draw the Universal Christ down through the crown of the head to flood the heart, then project it from the brow and visualize the building up of a large sphere or star of white light. This can be released into the hands of the Hierarchy of Light, with the request that it be used within God's Will and for the highest good of mankind. Spirit will then place it where it is needed.

We may envisage a scale of higher command on the heavenly planes. The analogy of warfare is often helpful. The directing power behind the great operation is the exalted being of the Christ, the Lord of the Elohim, the Son of God. Michael the great archangel, and now Time Spirit of the age, is his Commander in Chief, ''Regent of the Heavenly Forces upon Earth.'' The angelic hosts are the invisible forces of the Light now combating the darkness which has possessed the earth. We mortals are offered the opportunity to become a kind of fifth column, a resistance movement in the enemy-occupied country. We may volunteer for this service—there are no conscripts in this army. Though we are weak and insignificant, we are nevertheless a vital factor in the whole operation. For, as already said, the Powers of Light may not intervene to the denial of our free will. Therefore, we must invoke them and voluntarily offer the point of entry into earth consciousness. We must never be discouraged by our insignificance. As in modern warfare, we can never judge the importance of the action of a small unit. The platoons of the Rifle Brigade, under young 2nd Lieutenants, held Calais for several days against the advance of Hitler's armored corps. All communication was broken, yet they held and were obliterated, but the delay they caused made the miracle of Dunkirk possible. So we must never decide that our efforts are unimportant. We may be being used in ways we cannot understand. It has been well said that "God plus one is a majority."

The Book of Revelation appears to have been written for that time when human consciousness would have reached that point when it could take the great step beyond egoism into a reuniting with the great Oneness. That time is now. Thus, we read in Revelation (12:7):

> *And there was war in heaven: Michael and his angels fought against the dragon, and the dragon fought and his angels, and prevailed not . . . and the great dragon was cast out into the earth . . . having great wrath, because he knoweth that he hath but a short time.*

Thus Michael, known as the Countenance of Christ, appears to be the great commander who prepares the way for the Second Coming—whatever that formidable event is going to mean.

We may accept that he is that power which is leading us forward into a change of consciousness, an inner transformation. The New World comes about through each individual taking responsibility and changing himself. Thus, Michael is also known as the Lord of the Cosmic Intelligence. We must see that intellect is the functioning of the brain, the fabulous organ for consciousness operating in the earth plane. But the brain must be seen not so much as an organ for secreting thoughts as for reflecting Ideas. The Ocean of Intelligence, a field of God-thought, of course preceded the forming of the physical brain. We may say that the convolutions of the Brain are formed by the convolutions of Cosmic Thought. The intellectual activity is associated chiefly with the left hemisphere of the brain—the masculine, analytical side. The right hemisphere includes the "feminine," more sensitive faculties of intuition which can apprehend the Living Whole. We have developed a terribly over-masculinated way of thinking in the last centuries. We cannot come into true relation with spiritual knowledge and the higher worlds if we do not open ourselves to this more feminine intuition. Here is the true male- female balance which our society so needs. Herein lies the great truth that the Deity is male-female in its nature. So also will the Higher Self be.

We see the grim phenomenon in our time of men with great intellects and great will power but quite devoid of heart. These are the monsters of cruelty who can perpetrate the deeds of torture and murder with which we are all too familiar. This shows the separative intellectual impulse degraded and carried to terrible extreme. Indeed, we recognize that the being known as Ahriman, from the name of the Persian Lord of Darkness, is desperately operative in our civilization. He is the denier of the spirit, the force of all negation. We must recognize satanic forces in the form of beings who strive to get hold of the human intellect and personality and build a culture which entirely denies the Spirit. We may see this Ahrimanic impulse at work in a medicine which treats the body merely as a machine, a psychology which fails to recognize the Higher Self of man, a financial system which does not know of money as a flow of spiritual power, an economic and social system geared to getting for self, an astronomy which does not reckon with Divinity in the Universe, indeed in all reductionist thinking.

We need to recognize that the satanic forces are not a single devil but a polarity. The other operative force is that of Lucifer, the Fallen Angel. He encourages ego-aggrandizement so that men strive to be as gods and rejoice in the glory of their own ideas. Lucifer is behind the lust for power so apparent today. These two complementary aspects are the tempters who brought about the Fall. The Ahrimanic and Luciferic beings now work to hinder and prevent the ascent and redemption of man through the Christ Impulse. There is great delusion and danger if we do not recognize this polarity of satanic forces strongly at work in our society and in our souls and minds. Indeed, we cannot run our present society without making use of them, but at our peril if we do not understand. Redemption comes when the Christ Impulse enters the heart to hold the two tempters in their proper place. This understanding was first put forward by Steiner, and it is one of the most important aspects of his teaching. If we do not grasp the dual nature of the satanic powers, then Lucifer can draw us into illusion and the drive for power, and Ahriman can have a field day in our present culture as denier of the Spirit in man and the universe. Even our New Age movements can be led astray if they have not awakened to the nature of the two tempters continually at work to possess the mind and soul of man. Steiner carved a thirty foot sculptural group for the Goetheanum, his center for Spiritual Science. It shows the figure of Christ holding Ahriman in his place in the darkness of matter, controlling Lucifer in his place in the darkness of matter and controlling Lucifer in the air above. He called it ''The Representative of Humanity.''

To the rescue of mankind comes Michael, Lord of the Cosmic Intelligence, which has now descended to earth and can live in human thinking. Ahriman strives to possess the cold brainbound intellect, and he is indeed diabolically clever. The Michael impulse shows itself in the awakening of what can be called "the thinking of the heart," an individualized intelligence which can intensify normal thinking so that it begins to blend with the being within form and so attain knowledge of the higher worlds.

The "eye of the mind" can be awakened to apprehend the etheric forces working in trees and plants, animals and man. This leads to a widening of consciousness which will make it possible for man to tap the reservoirs of knowledge and eternal wisdom. The heart is the organ of the Spiritual Sun. In the heart, the Christ may be born again. This is the true Second Coming — that in one soul after another, the Christ Power may become a reality, over-spilling in Love and Light.

Yet the true step forward must come through the initiative of each of us. Thus, Michael beckons us on. He whispers in the still small voice. He will not now appear with Flaming Sword before us. Who would not follow him if he saw such a vision? Here is the great challenge, that we must individually wake up to the reality of Michael as the Countenance of the Christ, and out of the impulse of our own heart, acknowledge him and begin to work for him. Outwardly, he will hardly acknowledge our endeavors. It has been wisely said that "Michael only nods." If we do a free deed, he will note it and just nod in encouragement. For we have the honor of being accepted as potential co-creators with God, now called on to take total responsibility for all we do and are. We have as a race "come of age" and are urged to see the meaning of the Michael Mystery.

I quote an invocation by the Rev. Adam Bittleston of the Christian Community:

> *Amid the storm of the world,*
> *In which our souls share*
> *We seek the fiery leader of the Angel-host,*
> *Michael, Lord of true human thinking.*
> *His sword of iron drives away fear*

> *Which would entangle and ensnare man's will—*
> *His radiant purposes can fill our souls*
> *With Light Divine when autumn darkens earth*
> *He leads to Christ, and fights for Christ, for ever;*
> *So may we follow him, and fight beside him,*
> *With our whole being's love, and thought, on fire.*

Steiner has called Michael "the Fiery Thought King of the Universe." He is the warrior spirit ever fighting the dragon, the Beast who is thrown down to earth after making war in heaven. As Lord of the Cosmic Intelligence, it has been his task to control and administer the vast ocean of living thinking poured out from the mind of God. But Christ has descended from the Heaven-world of the Sun to redeem the planet Earth, the field of fallen humanity. The effect of the deed of Christ is to awaken in man the true sense of the spiritual "ego," the eternal divine spark in each of us. Michael, it appears, has followed the Christ by releasing the Cosmic Intelligence, that it may also descend to Earth and be taken up by man in transforming his intellect into an instrument for risen thinking that can apprehend and comprehend the supersensible.

The goal of evolution may be seen as the development of a being who could carry the gift of freedom and, thus, in due time, become a co-creator with God—a point in creation which itself becomes creative, thus releasing untold possibilities for development of untapped potential.

Planet Earth has become a seed point for a new impulse in the Universe. Michael's Cosmic Intelligence was essential for the overcoming of the limitations of sensebound, ego-bound thinking in man. The intellect, operating in the left hemisphere of the brain, proved a marvelous instrument for controlling and analyzing nature and thus building a great technology and materialistic culture, but the price was inevitably the atrophying of the subtler organs of perception. Thus man achieved freedom through loss of the spirit and allowed Ahriman to work in him to deny its very existence. That set the stage for an evolutionary step which may lead to the birth of a new type or species of humanity. The Cosmic Intelligence, released to man, awakened the possibility of a "thinking of the heart" which could, with love, perceive the supersensible within all forms of nature. Earth is called the Planet of Wisdom, and with our intellect, we can grasp the incredible wisdom built into every living form. But it needs awakened faculties

> *To see a World in a grain of sand*
> *And a Heaven in a wild flower*
> *To hold Infinity in the palm of your hand*
> *And Eternity in an hour.*

So wrote Blake, who also said:

> *If the doors of perception were cleansed, everything*
> *would appear to man as it is - infinite . . .*

This lost vision is being restored to us. The Michaelic task is to turn this planet of Wisdom into a planet of Love, for, once the vision is awakened, we begin to experience that the Deity in us is looking into the same divinity within the flower or the eyes of animal or fellow human, and it must needs love itself in the other.

This experience is Michael at work in our consciousness. Michael will regain the Lordship of the Cosmic Intelligence as man allows it to awaken in his redeemed thinking. We are to give it back to him in freedom, when it will flower in a new and wonderful way. Michael may not enforce this on us, since freedom is absolutely respected. Thus, he is a taciturn spirit, watching and waiting till we of our own initiative take the step into supersensible vision and holistic thinking. We come to see that Michaelic thinking will actually bring to birth a new psycho-spiritual organ in the central nervous system which will truly balance the workings of the two hemispheres of the brain. The new Michaelic humanity will hold a potential for evolutionary development into a species no longer merely earth-bound, but capable of sense-free thinking that can consciously enter the realms of spirit and work with the great angelic beings. Mankind, the 10th Hierarchy, is to take its place in creative harmony with the angelic worlds. This redemption of thinking through the awakening of the cosmic intelligence is the gateway to the New Epoch, when man, directly inspired by the Divine, will cooperate in bringing to birth "a new heaven and a new earth."

We know that Christ is with us always on the invisible, etheric plane. We must also recognize that Michael is ever present, urging us on into our true humanity. We must each of us awaken to this knowledge that in the immediate, ever-fleeting NOW, the Michaelic beings are there to lift us out of the morass of materialistic, matter-bound thinking. New worlds of light open up as consciousness is lifted and redeemed. The quantum leap is open to every one in this immediate moment, "the intersection point of the timeless with time."

We should be courageous to acknowledge that the New Age Movement is essentially Michaelic in its nature. The holistic world view, and with it the "alternative lifestyle" now emerging, is channelling the cosmic intelligence and awakening the heart center to cooperation and compassion. In the chapter on the Buddha and the Christ, I make the point that the Bodhisattva Manjushri and the Archangel Michael appear to be the same angelic beings, Lords of the Cosmic Intelligence. It in no way militates against the specific beliefs and aims of any branch of our movement to acknowledge Michael as the archangel overlighting the birth of a new civilization. All our work is in his service and under his inspiration.

Since he is also the Time Spirit of our epoch, it would be right to review Michaelmas as one of the great Festivals of the Year. Our year is divided by the Festivals like a great cross.

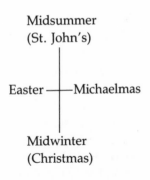

Midsummer
(St. John's)

Easter —— Michaelmas

Midwinter
(Christmas)

At the midwinter solstice, the earth's energies are withdrawn. Nature sleeps, but earth intelligence is most awake, waiting in suspense and watching during the Twelve Holy Nights. When Epiphany is passed, the sap again begins to rise and the earth moves forward to the feast of Resurrection at Easter.

The Summer Solstice is the time of outbreath for the forces of earth. While growth is active, the consciousness of earth may be more dormant, but earth is then more closely linked in its energies with the Cosmos. Thus, midsummer is a feast for poetry, music, dance and fire. The old pagan rituals carry secrets which are very relevant to the esoteric knowledge which lies behind exoteric Christianity.

Michaelmas is a festival as yet largely unrecognized and unformed. This is as it should be. Till our time, it has not had its full significance. With the maturing of mankind to spiritual adulthood, this is the festival of individual responsibility for the awakened ego of man joining with others in united soul endeavor. Ours is a time of new groupings, the forming of new communities and cooperative ventures. This is right and inevitable, for as we awaken to the reality of our higher self and of the Cosmic I AM working within each of us, we can lift consciousness and recognize each other human being as brother and sister. The One Life in infinite diversity animates every form, tree and plant, rock and cloud, animal and human. So we must come together for the realization of our own individual potential in service of the Whole. Since mankind is being forced to recognize One Earth, and since our self-made problems are on a planetary scale involving communal effort, it was inevitable that the first experiments of the collective under the Nazi and Marxist doctrine should have assumed that the individual must be sacrificed for the good and power of the state.

Our spiritual world view shows that when individuals come together to serve the whole for the glory of God, then the real needs are met out of the Divine abundance. Furthermore, the full creative talent of each individual is called forth and flowers in giving of his work. Thus the new collective founded on spiritual vision is a setting in which the full potential of the individual is called forth. In Teilhard de Chardin's powerful phrase, it demonstrates "Totalization without depersonalization." This is a supreme hope and joy. Inevitably, people are drawn together into new groups and communities. But each in service to the whole can be fulfilled by giving of and developing his particular talents.

So we are called on to devise a new kind of Michaelmas Festival to express united soul endeavor and the impulse for individual cooperation in creating new social forms which can be the vehicle for the ego that is open to the workings of its Higher Self. From our own heightened consciousness and dedicated endeavor, a society begins to form which can veritably channel the Christ impulse. To this goal the Michaelmas Festival must point, and we are free to create it in any way that expresses these truths.

A new significance is found in the pilgrimage to the centers dedicated to St. Michael. In medieval days, such holy places as Mont St. Michel and St. Michael's Mount were focal points for streams of pilgrims, and we are beginning to realize what power must have been circulating along the great pilgrimage routes. If only some of the great streaming of tourists could be converted into genuine pilgrimage in our own time, much power for world healing would undoubtedly be generated. Modern discoveries about ley lines and the existence of power points and light centers give us a new vision of the deep reality underlying the choice of the ancient sites. Indeed, the revelations of modern dowsing are showing that the sacred temples and churches were often sited on points of earth power. The Living Earth is an organism with its own blood stream and breathing of forces and etheric energies. Ancient Wisdom clearly knew about this invisible reality, and sensitives could experience that at certain places the Power was flowing and could be tapped and channelled. The sensitive, Grace Cooke, in her book *Light over Britain*, describes her visionary experiences in which she saw Stonehenge and Avebury as temples for storing the spiritual light. It is as if the temples and holy mountains were generating points from which the healing power could be drawn along the ley lines, as we now spread electric power along our straight lines of pylons. Thus, we may believe that the many churches dedicated to St. Michael and all Angels represent points for grounding and contacting the cosmic power and light. Cornwall and Brittany and the Celtic areas are rich in such centers. The adept, Tudor Pole, urged the importance of deliberate pilgrimage with a simple ritual of invocation, procession, music, poetry and light as a means of activating the dormant power in these centers. We should always greet the guardian of any holy place when we visit it and give thanks on leaving. It is not mere archaic fantasy to feel that St. Michael's Mount and Mont St. Michel are truly centers for the flowing of the powers of earth and heaven.

Let us close this chapter with the great prayer to Michael found by Tudor Pole and credited to Eusebius in about A.D. 200.

Ye hosts angelic by the high archangels led,
Heavenly powers beneficent
Mighty in the Music of the Word,
Great ones entrusted with the sovereignty
Of infinite celestial spheres
Marshalling the Cherubim and the flaming Seraphim,
Ye O Michael Prince of Heaven
And Gabriel by whom the Word is given,
Uriel, great archangel of the Earth,

Raphael of healing ministry to those who yet in bondage are,
Guide our footsteps as we journey onward
Into light eternal.

6 | The Buddha and the Christ

THE AGELESS WISDOM recognizes the vast Oneness of all life. Mankind is an integral part of this oneness. The ensouled body is indeed the bridge between the physical and ethereal worlds. In our lower limbs, we reach down into the gravity field of earth, while the lifted head poised on the upright spine is open to the thought of the Cosmos. It is like a chalice for receiving the inpouring of Divine Light. The Universe, as Jeans saw, comes to look less and less like a mechanism and more like a great Thought. This all the ancient religions knew. All is Spirit, and matter is frozen spirit, just as ice is water consolidated.

Since the great religions are expressions of these stupendous truths, and since their teachings must be directed to redeeming mankind from the sense of separation from the whole, we must expect them to present facets of the Oneness picture and thus to stand together in a complementary manner. The conflicts which abound in world history are but distortions of the truth. Thus Buddhism and Christianity, in their true depth, must be closely linked. It is not a question of simply choosing the prophet we like best, but of recognizing how Truth plays through great impulses which lift mankind out of the suffering directly caused by deviation from the Divine Law.

The Buddha has been described as the greatest and holiest man that ever lived, the spirit incarnate of absolute self-sacrifice, of all the highest virtues attainable on this earth of sorrow. He taught the path to enlightenment and the way out of suffering. In achieving enlightenment, he experienced the ocean of Life and Light which is indeed open to all men. Buddhism is a teaching of the way to enlightenment. It is rightly not a "religion" as such, but a path from ignorance to enlightenment. The Buddha always refused to discuss the "indeterminates," since his teaching of the Way was all-important. Therefore, he is not concerned with God but with the overcoming of the twin evils of Ignorance and the Thirst for Life which binds mankind into the morass of illusion in the world of appearance and form.

Life in embodiment leads to egoism and the sense of separation and individuality. To the Buddhist, this is the great illusion. When Knowledge and Enlightenment have been achieved, the consciousness will blend again into the Whole. The Buddha achieved unity with the Ocean of Thought and Wisdom from which all separated forms have derived and to which all must return. Nirvana is this condition of Oneness attained. All human suffering is the direct result of the thirst for life and the illusion of separate identity. To overcome this is the way to the relief of suffering. How important is this goal in our modern world!

The teaching of the Oneness of all life and of compassion for all beings implies that our real Self is one with the ALL. TAT TVAM ASI—THAT ART THOU, is the great doctrine of the Orient, whether in Hindu or Buddhist teaching. To meditate until we can know in what sense we *are* the flower, the tree, the bird or the other human soul—this is the goal and the way. We have no real separate identity. That is illusion in a plane which is Maya.

The direct result of this vision is profound sympathy for all living things. There is absolute toleration within the whole structure of Buddhism, and there have been no wars between its doctrinal branches. No blood has ever been shed over disputes on dogma. Would that this could be said of the history of Christianity or of Islam! Thus, the present extending of the influence of Buddhism over the world and into the West may prove to be a harmonious factor of immense importance in the tensions of the next decades.

The Buddha released a teaching of the path to enlightenment and compassion. Cease to do evil. Learn to do good. Cleanse your own heart. Such is the teaching, and his dying words were, "Work out your salvation with diligence." We may compare this with the motto of the Grail Knights—"Work on yourself and serve the world."

The Christ has said: I am the Light of the World

I am the Life

I am Love

The Buddha teaches the way into Light—the way into that Source which *is* the Christ. As at one time Buddha gave the world the teaching of love and Light, so at another Christ brought Love itself as a living force and power into the world. The two deeds are complementary. The Buddha under the Bodhi tree received Enlightenment. This supreme event will compare with the Baptism of Jordan when the perfected man, Jesus, received the cosmic individuality, the exalted Being of Light.

Christ is much more than a teacher. He brings a Divine force into the world for the redemption of fallen Man. His descent into the stream of human evolution was essential if mankind were to survive. His entry into the realm of matter and his passage through death and resurrection was like an injection of eternal life into the human system. Since then it becomes possible for each human being to find the Christ within the living forces of the earth and to awaken His Love as a transforming force within the heart.

If we are able to accept the world view implicit in esoteric Christianity, we shall get a better understanding of the relation of our religion to Buddhism. The two streams of esoteric and exoteric Christianity run parallel with each other through history. They are not in essential conflict and the one can and will illumine the other. But alas, the esoteric knowledge held in the first centuries by the followers of Christ was driven underground as heresy when the Church became universal in the Roman Empire. Obvi-

ously, the esoteric doctrines and teachings were much too difficult for the general mass of believers, for they are closely related
to the mystery knowledge taught in the Temples of Initiation.
Furthermore, they implied and still imply the possibility for the
individual soul to make direct contact in the heart with Christ
Himself, without the intermediary of the priest. This, in those
early days, could not be allowed, so the knowledge was repressed as heresy and driven underground. It was carried forward by the Knights Templar, by the Cathars and Albigenses,
who were cruelly suppressed and exterminated, and later by the
Rosicrucian impulse and the Freemasons. The same knowledge
re-emerges in our century as a central aspect of the Ageless Wisdom. It involves the recognition of the Cosmic Christ as the Exalted Being of all Light, the Lord of the Elohim, Son of God, overlighting all men of every blood and creed. Spiritual research finds
His descent at the Baptism of Jordan into the prepared human
vehicle of Jesus to be the turning point of history. With the flowing of the Divine Blood of Golgotha, the impulse of renewal and
regeneration penetrated the vital forces of the whole earth. The
redemptive deed of Christ in passing through death and so entering into the stream of earth evolution reverses the Fall and starts
the Ascent of Man. Our deeper imagining will grasp the profound workings of destiny to bring about this epoch-making
event. It was foreseen by all the great religions.

The Cosmic Christ, by whatever name, overlights all mankind.
It cannot but be that the great beings on the higher planes were all
united in preparing for the consummation of this great deed.
Thus, the great soul of Gotama must have made its descent to
earth in the knowledge of the impulse of love which was to follow
600 years later. And now these exalted beings must surely be
working together for the redemption of mankind at this critical
turning point at the end of the twentieth century.

Hence the significance of the Wesak Festival at the May full
moon. We are becoming ever more aware of the importance of the
three linked festivals at the Full Moons of April, May and June.

They are occasions for the inflowing of cosmic power, and they call for a united act of invocation. The first is, of course, the Easter Festival of the Resurrection; the second is the Wesak; and the third is the Christ Festival of World Invocation. The Wesak celebrates a unity of the Buddhic and Christ impulses. It is said to take place in a hidden Himalayan Valley to which many pilgrims are drawn from all nations and races. It is clearly an esoteric mystery. The Christ Being and the Masters, known as the Hierarchy, foregather, and at the moment of the Full Moon, the Buddha descends from the heights of Wisdom and Enlightenment, appearing as a great figure of light out of the heavenly heights, to bless mankind and unite his compassion and wisdom with the Love and Power of the Christ. Present also is the Master, Jesus, now the head of the ''Hierarchy'' of the great masters. It is believed that these great men, who for many centuries have not needed to take on physical incarnation, will in our time be appearing in our midst in human form, to teach mankind and to prepare for the great Coming of the Christ. For this momentous event, as we have seen, is the purpose and meaning of our apocalyptic age. Whatever the meaning of this symbolism, we must surely feel how closely united is the Buddhist stream with that of esoteric Christianity, for the Supreme Oneness of Life and Light is present in the enlightenment of the Buddha and the redemptive deed of Christ.

A further parallel of great interest is found in the teachings of Patanjali, the great follower and interpreter of the Buddha, some 300 years after his death. The symbol of the Wheel of Life has been much used in painting and architectural carving. The outer rim of the wheel is shown as the area of illusion in the material world, and the eight spokes represent the Noble Eight-fold Path leading man ultimately to the hub of the Wheel which symbolizes Nirvana. Patanjali develops this to represent the sixteen Yogas which, taken together in his teaching, cover the full path to enlightenment.

It is fascinating, however, to find that Patanjali's Wheel of Life is almost identical with the Essene Tree of Life. The Essenes, we remember, based their teachings on the knowledge gained by Moses, and this leads back to Enoch and to the ancient Zoroaster of Persia. Moses discovered the One Law and experienced the oceans of Life, of Wisdom, Love and Power which were omni-present throughout the universe. These he called the Angels, in order to imply fields of force and energy which were also alive and self-activating. His discoveries are later reflected in the vision of the Nine Angelic Hierarchies. These oceans of divine energy are surely identical with those found by the Buddha in his en-lightenment. They are also being rediscovered by the advanced physicists in our time who come to the unitary picture of the uni-verse and know it as a vast continuum of creative consciousness. The Essenes recognized fourteen primary fields of energy, seven of the earthly Mother and seven of the Heavenly Father. Compare these with the sixteen Yogas of Patanjali arranged around the Wheel of Life in two rings representing the Noble eight-fold Outer Path and the Noble eight-fold Inner Path, with the eight spokes leading to the central hub of Nirvana. Must we not feel that these two teachings tap the same Source?

Thus:

Patanjali	*Essene Tree of Life*
	Communions with the Angels
Outer Rings of Yogas	*of the Earthly Mother*
1 Earth	1 Earthly Mother
2 Man	2 Soil, Seeds, Regeneration
3 Health	3 Life
4 Joy	4 Joy
5 Sun	5 Sun
6 Water	6 Water
7 Air	7 Air
8 Food	

Inner Ring of Yogas	*Communions with the Angels of the Heavenly Father*
1 Creation	1 Heavenly Father
2 Eternal Life	2 Eternal Life
3 Work	3 Creative Work
4 Peace	4 Peace
5 Power	5 Power
6 Love	6 Love
7 Wisdom	7 Wisdom
8 Preservation	

Here is yet another interesting parallel. Steiner wrote his important book *Knowledge of the Higher Worlds: How is it Achieved?* giving his teachings on meditation and the approaches to higher consciousness drawn from his own spiritual researches as scientist/seer. An oriental sage declared that nothing in Steiner's book in any way conflicts with the teachings of Patanjali.

He has a chapter on the opening of the throat chakra, the psychic center concerned with clairvoyance. There are, of course, short cuts to extended vision and psychic experience, such as drugs or dabbling in the black arts. The result of such practices will be that the ''petals'' of the lotus center may partially open, resulting in delusion, and the soul's progress may be gravely impaired. Thus, he emphasizes the basic esoteric law that for every step in spiritual knowledge, the student must see to it that he takes three steps in the training of character. This obviously precludes the short cuts for which the motive may be personal power. For the true opening of the throat center involved what Steiner called the eight functions of the soul. These correspond exactly with Buddha's Eight-fold Path of Right Thinking, Right Intention, Right Speech, Right Action, Right Management of Life, Right Endeavor, Right Mindfulness, Right Self-observation. So here again, the Christo-centric teaching of Steiner proves to be close to that of Buddhism. A basic harmony exists since the same truth underlies both.

Now let us consider the Buddhist attitude towards reincarnation, since the interest in this theme is now very wide. We have seen how it is taught that the thirst for life and the satisfying of desire draws man down to earth and binds him to sense experience. If all is Thought, and thoughts are alive, and in everything we are united with the All, then the quality of our thinking will draw us together with beings of kindred emphasis. Thus, if we choose to think thoughts of fear, greed and hate, we shall be bound ever closer to similar fields of thought. If we can lift our thinking to the eternal values of light, courage, hope and joy, we shall be ever increasingly drawn up towards the Eternal planes. Through redemption of thinking lies the way to knowledge, and our own salvation is in our own hands. The Buddhist sees that negative thinking binds mankind to the illusory world of the self and of material appearance and that he will, therefore, experience an endless round of existences within the gravity field until he can overcome the thirst for life and lift to the eternal plane which leads ultimately to Nirvana. This brings freedom from the need to incarnate.

Now we must acknowledge that the West has a concern with individuality which is unacceptable and even incomprehensible to the East. Furthermore, the concept of reincarnation as it reappeared in the West is fundamentally different from that held in the East. It is by no means a mere taking over of an Eastern teaching. For the West is imbued with an evolutionary vision and a profound concern with life on earth. Indeed, the Christian vision would not see the realm of matter as in itself mere illusion from which we must escape. We begin to glimpse the wonder and the miracle of physical creation. But we ourselves are responsible for bringing about the illusion that it is spiritless and consists of an infinite number of separate things. Our task is to overcome *that* illusion and re-experience what we begin to know as the truth— that Spirit informs all matter, that Being interpenetrates all things and that we can each rise above the limitations of sense-bound thinking and merge in consciousness with the Whole. The Fall of Man represents a loss of vision of the spiritual nature of the Universe and man. Our redemption is made possible through the deed of Christ.

God declared to Moses: "I AM THAT I AM." The I AM is the great Cosmic Individuality and our own Higher Self is an attribute of it. Thus, if the soul can free itself from its illusory subpersonalities, it can reach up to its own Higher Self, Christ-filled. It is within our own thinking that the inner voice speaks "BE STILL AND KNOW THAT I AM GOD."

Since the descent of the Christ, the possibility has been given to us of developing a true Individuality (the very word means the "Undividedness"). We begin to see that the entity within each of us, that which can say "I," is an eternal droplet of the Divine Ocean, and that potentially it can evolve into a being who can be a co-creator with God. And the purpose of incarnation upon earth is to take part in the great task of raising consciousness to ever higher levels so that in due time all the spirit imprisoned in matter and form can be redeemed. Thus, the human being, as the crown of evolution who can bear and carry the gift of free will and rational consciousness, has a major role to play in this huge cosmic drama. A wider picture of evolution emerges. Physical evolution is the outer working of a long spiritual operation through which the original archetype, created by God in the beginning, is realized in its ultimate perfection upon earth. Man, last to appear in physical form, is first as Archetypal Idea, made in the image of God.

Thus, as organisms develop from the primal slime and the bodily forms evolve to increasing consciousness, there comes a time when the spiritual entity, the I Being, can enter the stream of evolution and embody itself. As physical evolution proceeds, a parallel spiritual process takes place: the entry of the "I" to take on a body, to lift and improve it and then return to the spiritual source for a while, to plunge again when time is ripe in order to share the next evolutionary step and with it the deepening of consciousness. In this view, each of us has had our share in the entire evolutionary process. It was Lessing who in 1780 presented his *Essay on the Education of the Human Race*, the first serious state-ment of a Western doctrine of reincarnation. He likened history to a school. In each epoch, there is new knowledge to learn and experience to be gained. Surely each soul must enter each period and learn its lessons. One sojourn cannot be adequate, any more than one term in a school's third form would qualify one to enter a university. Thus he concludes that all developing souls must have passed through each historical period, and there must be further to go. There is no end to the process. Once on the path, adult education will never cease and the interest will heighten as we open soul and mind to wider and higher fields of conscious-ness. Lessing ended with the majestic phrase—"Is not the whole of Eternity mine?"

Thus, in the West, with our feeling for the reality of the "I," the concept of reincarnation takes the form of a creative deed of im-mense interest and significance. It is by no means a mere drag-ging back through desire to the melancholy shell of life which is to be escaped as soon as possible. It is a sublime process of educa-tion and creative art in which mankind shares in the redemption of the planet, lifting himself out of the self-created illusion of the personality to unite with the eternal I AM in which lives the power and Being of the Cosmic Christ.

Admittedly, the whole concept of repeated earth lives is very complex, and clearly it is very difficult for our earth-bound intel-lects to grasp and understand it; but we may take it that Earth is the great training ground for souls and that the goal is the pro-gressive widening of consciousness till this can encompass the width of the cosmic oceans. For the potential of Man is vast. The goal is not merely that the drop should flow into the ocean but the greater mystery that somehow the ocean can flow into the drop.

And here is an important point which we can take if we will

look at History as a sweep of evolving consciousness. The soul condition of man itself evolves. It is the greatest fallacy to think that "human nature doesn't change."

Oriental consciousness has remained simply unconcerned with individuality, for its striving has been directed always towards the Oversoul. In the West where concern has been strongly directed into the material world, acute self-consciousness has been developed and with it now the vision of the I AM, the Higher Self, the eternal Individuality. This soul condition, called by Steiner the Consciousness Soul, is a recent development in the centuries following the Renaissance. It is our task to develop this form of cognition. It could not exist in earlier epochs nor in the oriental setting. There is, therefore, no question of one view being right and the other wrong, any more than it is "wrong" for Autumn to have no daffodils or for England to grow oaks instead of palm trees. Both views are right in their age and place, for they are complementary aspects of the One Truth. It is only our too logical thinking that will see any essential conflict, since as aspects of the Whole, the two views are in harmony and, indeed, support and illumine each other. Christ and Buddha can never be opposed, and if they appear to be, it is because of our limited understanding or a debasing of their true teaching and impulse.

The spiritual destiny of the West has been to focus attention on the world of matter. Seen in this way, there is nothing wrong with materialism. The human lot has certainly been improved and suffering reduced. It goes wrong and becomes evil when getting more things and satisfying more desires becomes an end in itself. Then, man deviates ever more from the law of Harmony and through his egosim brings down disaster and suffering upon himself. The purification of the motive is the great need. The redemption of the earth calls for a turnabout in consciousness, and here surely the marriage of the Buddhist teaching with the Western spiritual world view would be immensely fruitful. It is, indeed, vital and essential for the very survival of mankind. The redemptive deed of Christ starts a process which leads through to the discovery of the I AM, the Higher Self within us. The illusion of personality and of the material world is transformed through this illumination of the I AM.

The Lords of Light overlight all mankind. We move towards One World Religion of Worship of the Light. There can be no essential conflict between the truth in each of the great religious world-conceptions.

This is not a case of choice of prophets, as has sometimes been assumed by broad-minded agnosticism. It was part of planned destiny that the Buddha should come 600 years before Christ to launch into the world the impulse to enlightenment and the teaching of the path of compassion for suffering. It was preplanned. The Celestial Team is working together to redeem mankind through love and by the force of Cosmic Intelligence.

Now *Manjushri*, the Bodhisattva of Wisdom, is the Lord of the Cosmic Intelligence, portrayed with his flaming sword to destroy ignorance and his scroll of the Ancient Wisdom. Intelligence is shown as the power which opens the "thinking of the heart." Is this not, in essence, the same being as the Archangel Michael? In the great allegory of the Apocalypse, Michael and his angels throw the Beast down to earth where he fights furiously "because he knoweth that his time is short." The Beast, the Lord of Darkness, Ahriman of Mephistopheles, is supremely clever and works to capture the brain-bound intellect, so that he may deny the spirit and drive it out of human consciousness. Manjushri/Michael overthrows him and "binds him a thousand years." They open the thinking of the heart, the true balance of male and female consciousness in mankind. Intuition and intellect work hand in hand to bring about the new renaissance.

In Fitzgerald's *Rubaiyat of Omar Khayyam*, we find the verse:

> *The Mighty Mahmud, the victorious Lord,*
> *Who all the misbelieving and black horde*
> *Of fears and sorrows that possess the soul*

Scatters and slays with his enchanted sword.

Replace "Mahmud" with "Michael" or "Manjushri" and here is the same truth.

> *Oh my Beloved, fill the Cup that clears*
> *Today of past regrets and future fears.*

If the Cup is seen in its mystical sense, is not this pure Buddhism, living in the Eternal Now, and pure Christianity, with the Chalice perhaps beginning to supercede the Cross as a symbol of our age of renewal? Today there is vast need for toleration and compassion. Can we see how the Buddhist impulse in its profound truth flows directly into the renewed Christianity—the teaching of love and the Power of Love itself? To many now will come the experience of Paul on the road to Damascus. The heart is opened with Love overspilling, and the soul knows that Christ Lives, that He is the Life and Light and Love to whom the Buddha leads us.

Negative egoism will be swept away. Operation Redemption is launched by the joined forces of the Light, all pointing to a true world religion of Worship of the Exalted Beings of Light.

The age invites a new eclecticism—the ability to draw on the many facets of the Truth and see them not as rival doctrines but complementary and fulfilling each other. There is no question of trying to disprove either the Buddhist view or the Christian. Both speak to aspects of our soul. Steiner himself once declared that: "Because the Buddha was right, the Christ had to come."

I close with another quotation from Leonora Nichols' *Within is the Fountain.* It seems so relevant to the theme of this chapter and speaks with high authority.

> *Revelation wipes out Time with all its accumulated ills and brings into focus the Eternal, the Divine.*

You are standing, at this timeless moment, in that Eternal Light, and what is that Light but the Radiance of Love itself? To feel this ecstatic Truth is to Be it, to partake of it.

The divine message of the Fountain of Light, as shown you in vision, was Love revealing itself, symbolically, for your understanding.

To experience Truth is to know it forever. We have led you to this moment of illumination that you may relate all that is to come to this Supreme Fact upon which Eternal Life rests: that the Source of your life, or all life, is *Love Itself*. This *One Truth* fulfills the *One Law*. When this is deeply understood and experienced as revelation, all else disappears.

7 | Finding the Inner Teacher

VERY RELEVANT to the holistic world picture is the emergence of "psychosynthesis" as a step beyond "psychoanalysis." And out of it has come "transpersonal psychology." Psychosynthesis involves a recognition of the Higher Self as a spiritual principle in mankind. Freud discovered the subconscious and believed that virtually all creative impulses were related to repression of sex. The great C. G. Jung developed the concept of the collective unconscious but was still wary of admitting to the higher self, though at the end of his life, in the B.B.C. interview, when asked if he believed in God, he made the now famous reply—"I do not believe—I know." Roberto Assagioli had the courage to shape the psychology of psychosynthesis on the positive belief that the Higher Self is a major factor in our being through which creative drives may come from the super-conscious. This is essentially an aspect of the recovery of the lost knowledge that man is a being of Spirit, Soul and Body. Assagioli's work was further developed by Maslow, Progoff and Frankl. The American universities have been more ready to recognize psychosynthesis, but till now in Britain, the concept of a Higher Self has been largely ignored or rejected in academic psychology on the grounds that it cannot be scientifically proven.

Thus, for an emergence of a spiritual world view, transpersonal psychology is of supreme importance, for it will relate to all the oriental and western techniques for meditation and self-mastery.

Within the New Age movement is appearing a new form of

counseling which will prove of real significance. So many people in need of help are wary of going to orthodox psychiatrists who may themselves be non-believers and may use drugs to repress symptoms which may well be aspects of break-through into a deeper spiritual understanding. We move into a period of dramatic change in society, in the Earth itself and inevitably within the psyche. We face the probability of a transformation in human consciousness before the end of the century as the necessary prelude to the entry into the Aquarian Age. Many people begin to experience a fourth-dimensional vision. A pressure appears to be coming which will dislodge us from the grounding of belief in the sole power of rational, logical intellect. We have to find the path to attaining knowledge of higher worlds through intuitive self-development. This is surely the destiny of modern man.

Dynamic change through break-down and break-through is going to need help towards synthesis of the psyche, and the finding of the true Self, the eternal spiritual aspect of our nature—"transpersonal" indeed.

We hardly know yet what qualifications are needed for true "Counseling." It is a new profession, and an academic degree in psychology alone is not the answer. An awakening of compassion and deeper sympathy, a training in transpersonal psychology and a knowledge of astrology will be tolls for the counsel. Mary Swainson's book on *The Spirit of Counsel* will be of help to many.

We are learning through the rigors of earth life to reach out towards our eternal being. This means that we choose to set our feet on the path leading to conscious submission and cooperation with the Divine Will, as it speaks through our Higher Self. This concept restores a sense of real meaning to our lives. It was Victor Frankl who first recognized, out of concentration camp experience, that so much mental and psychological breakdown came from loss of sense of meaning in life. Thus he evolved what he called Logotherapy, which means healing through restoring meaning. We learn that Earth is truly the training ground of the soul and that all trials and tribulations may be experienced as a tempering of the soul so that it may move through into the eternal planes of higher consciousness. Thus, we are passing through a critical phase of soul-education. There is indeed no end to adult education on this plane or the next, and, in this sense, the prospects beyond the darkness are bright indeed.

With the spiritual awakening in our century, it is inevitable that many have turned to the East in quest of the guru or teacher, since the Orient has worked and lived for spiritual development through centuries of unbroken training. The West has in the last four centuries been involved with the mastery of the physical world and this has led to our great materialist civilization at the price of losing knowledge of the spiritual nature of the human being. It is interesting that when Warren Hastings, at the end of the eighteenth century, introduced the first translation of the Baghavad Gita into Western Europe, it took the intellectual society by storm in revealing that there was in the East a path to knowledge wholly different from our Western reliance on the active masculine intellect. By turning inward in meditation and working on the self to tame the wayward mind and transmute desire, consciousness can be released to explore into the wise realms of spiritual understanding.

So, inevitably and rightly enough, Westerners have sought out the Eastern gurus. The really wise ones always showed that their goal was not personal power but the desire to lead the student through to the discovery that the source of knowledge and guidance lay within himself.

Browning expresses this finely in the opening lines of his *Paracelsus*:

> *Truth is within ourselves. It takes no rise*
> *From outward things whate'er you may believe.*
> *There is an inmost center in us all*
> *Where Truth abides in fullness, but around*

> *Wall upon wall the gross flesh hems it in*
> *This perfect clear perception, which is Truth. . . .*

In the last years the emphasis has moved ever more strongly onto the importance of finding the Inner Teacher, so that, taking ever fuller responsibility for ourselves, we have less need to rely on the outer guru.

The Higher Self speaks in "the still small voice" within our own thinking. It is as if we answered our own question within our own thought. But our busy chattering minds are so noisy that we rarely hear, though the I AM is speaking quietly to us all the time. Until we really still ourselves and listen, there is no hope of our hearing. Here lies the profound importance of regular meditation—to still the body, emotions and mind and to listen with relaxed but alert attention, so that we may hear the words or apprehend the thought-form from the Beyond. What a delicate and beautiful arrangement, through which the Source of all Power can gently communicate without in any way interfering with our freedom. We are always perfectly free to reject its guidance, since we appear to have given it to ourselves.

Our Higher Self is indeed an attribute of God. It is the spiritual aspect of our being and is one with the spiritual continuum. Thus the Inner Teacher is, in a real sense, speaking with the Voice of God. This does not mean that we have a hot line to the Almighty Himself, any more than that every letter addressed to the Prime Minister is replied to by that august personage, even though it is signed in his or her name. But we know that the angelic hierarchies are all integrally part of the thought of God. We contact the Divine Realm through our High Self and our angel. An exalted Being wishing to communicate with the human level will need to relay his message down through a number of stages, for to reach our mundane consciousness involves a lowering of vibration. We must learn to judge by the quality of the communication whether it is genuinely light-filled. The mind in meditation may be richly filled with thoughts which come both from angelic beings and our own beloved friends who have left the body and are attuned to us through affinity.

The greatest of the Inner Teachers has said: "I am with you always, even to the end of the Earth cycle."

Inner communications may speak as if they are from God or the Christ, and the Higher Self is indeed the individual channel to these great sources. Thus, the finding and attuning to the Inner Teacher is the major task and is essential to the purpose of our life on earth. The experience of separation gives the setting for this soul achievement, the overcoming of individual self-hood and egoism in order to reunite consciously and in freedom with the Divine. This is the whole "object of the exercise." As Rhadakrishnan wrote,

> *The oldest wisdom in the world tells us that we can consciously unite with the divine whilst in the body; for this man is really born. If he misses his destiny, Nature is not in a hurry; she will catch him up someday and compel him to fulfill her secret purpose.*

A quickening of the spirit is now taking place. An operation for the redemption of mankind has been launched. The inflooding of the Christ Power must, of course, be through individual souls, and here there will be no constraint or compulsion. It must be a free giving of self to Self. Thus each human being is vital for the great renewal. We may through ignorance or indifference choose to close ourselves, and then the power will pass us by. But if we respond, then at once the fountain flow can begin, and this will purge and cleanse and wash away the negative and dark in us and allow us to become channels for the impulse of renewal. It is a great rebirth that is starting now, a new dawn of the Sun that rises upon all creatures from within.

So we see the purpose of meditation, and it is profound. Unless we learn to create an inner center of stillness, the Higher Voice cannot reach us. The initiative is always ours. Nothing can happen unless we choose.

"Behold I stand at the door and knock."

If we can open, then indeed the transformation can begin. It is an adventure into inner worlds. And it aligns us with the immense operation now afoot for building the world anew.

The Voice speaks: BE STILL AND KNOW THAT I AM GOD.

Here is the greatest of all injunctions. Our personal "I am" can open itself to Him who said I AM THAT I AM. And we learn to know that the I AM, the great Cosmic Being, the Beloved, is personalized for us through our Higher Self.

The goal of man on earth is to find GOD and surrender the personal self wholly to the Impersonal Self, the transpersonal Divinity. Here lies the greatest of paradoxes in a life made up of paradox: if we can really surrender all and submit to God's will, then we know the truth that "His service is perfect freedom."

It seems as if now an ever greater pressure is being brought to bear on us to make this surrender and put ourselves wholly under His direction, guided in the moment by inner intuition (tuition from within). This would be the clue enabling us to move creatively through change.

We may prevent ourselves from finding the inner teacher if we are too tied down to a preconceived structure of belief. All the great religions present facets of the Truth. Doctrine and dogma may be relevant to a period and may well hold sublime aspects of Truth, but none can have the whole. It is as if Truth were an immense many-faceted crystal, our vision of it perpetually widening. It is too easy to seek security in our castle of belief. These fortresses, so necessary at a certain stage, tend to become dungeons. The lightly-used phrase "freedom of thought" may turn out to be the freedom to continue to imprison ourselves in our old structure of belief, thus preventing the leap in awareness.

It may be that now, in this time of dissolution and aquifer (a modern Reformation), many will be called on to adventure into the totally new, under immediate guidance from the Higher Self.

It could be like a kind of commando operation, traveling light into change, jettisoning all superfluous possessions and beliefs. Many of us have had some sort of training in our chosen path or discipline which will prove to be an essential foundation. NOW we may have to learn to go forward with no labels or sets of "beliefs."

To quote from an inspired little book, *The Impersonal Life*, in which the I AM addresses the reader:

> *The time has arrived, if you can but see it, when you cast aside all accumulated knowledge, all teaching, all religions, all authority . . . for I have quickened you to the consciousness of My Presence within, to the fact that all authority, teachings and religions, coming from any outer source, no matter how lofty or sacred, can no longer have any influence with you, except as they become a means of turning you within to Me, for My final authority on all questions of whatsoever nature.*

"Leave all and follow Me," has manifold meaning. The challenge of the coming years implies that we must all learn the art of living courageously and creatively into change. We are bound to be faced with situations that have no precedent, and there are certain to be very difficult adjustments to make. The normal reaction to sudden demands and moments of crisis will be to revert to old habit patterns and brain tracks. But these may be as little use to us as the splendid instincts of a tiger would be if it were let loose in Piccadilly in a rush hour. How then do we prepare for moving through change into the unknown?

The answer lies in the recognition of the Inner Guidance of the Higher Self. We are always shown one step ahead—but usually only one. Much of our anxiety and worry arises from our trying to look ten steps ahead. The immediate moment, let us admit it, is rarely intolerable. The agony often comes from remorse about the past and anxiety about the future.

O my beloved, fill the Cup that clears
Today of past regrets and future fears.

The real adventure starts when the point of no return is passed and there is absolute committal, and faculties are stretched to the uttermost, whether it be in the great sports, in the crafts or in warfare. Escaping from a prison camp, there would be no choice but to live absolutely in the instant, throwing oneself wholly onto the guidance of intuition with absolute obedience. Read Frederic Lionel's book *Challenge* in which he describes his four years in the French Resistance Movement. This, he came to realize, amounted to a training in absolute reliance on the guidance of his higher self and the mysterious workings of intuition. When the changes really come upon us, we shall all need ever-increasingly to learn to live thus in the moment. This would be a reckless gamble if the materialist world view were the only truth, but it may prove to be an essential aspect of the lifestyle of those who recognize the ever-present reality of the spiritual worlds. It may seem as if we are lost in a maze or crossing a bog in the night on stepping stones. We may have to learn to throw ourselves bravely on the momentary guidance of the Higher Self. "One step enough for me," was Newman's dictum. Life could become something like a lighthearted game with destiny. We may be certain our invisible guides and our friends out of the body will rally to help us in times of pressure. Let us learn to work with them, for they have a wider view of events than we who are still involved with the labyrinth. The inner voice of intuition will be equivalent to Ariadne's thread. We are already under training in preparation for the times of greater stress. We have here, perhaps, a real clue to a technique for living into change and avoiding what has been called "Future Shock," and this understanding arises directly out of thinking ourselves into the spiritual world view.

We all know those moments when, with a sudden gush of joy in the heart, we get a flash of vision of a new course of action, a bubbling up of enthusiasm for some new way forward—"Oh how lovely, what fun that would be." Then the cold reason steps in and says "Oh no, you can't do that. It would cost too much and everyone would think it silly." So, through thinking too precisely on the event, enterprises of great pith and moment turn their currents awry and lose the name of action.

Such momentary flashes may be the speaking of the Inner Teacher. (Enthusiasm, after all, means "possessed by a god.") But inevitably, the inspired course of action will involve doing something quite contrary to old habit patterns. Thus, we may be called on to act into the Higher Self— literally to *act* a part we have never rehearsed. Then if we bravely take the plunge, the invisible worlds will respond instantly by pouring in energy, and we may find we have done or said things we could never have conceived before. It is not for nothing that Englishmen are the finest race of amateur actors. Perhaps here is a true use of this faculty.

The High Self stages trials and situations, allowing us free rein to hurt ourselves and to follow our whims and desires, our ambitions and self-aggrandizement, until ultimately, disillusioned, we turn and come back to Him as He waits within.

He is indeed the Hound of Heaven:

> *But with unhurrying chase,*
> *And unperturbèd pace,*
> *Deliberate speed, majestic instancy,*
> *Come on the following Feet*
> *And a Voice above their beat—*
> *Naught shelters thee who wilt not shelter me.*

When once we see that the One Father/Mother God is working in the High Self of everyone, controlling the whole great pattern and waiting for us at last to wake up and put ourselves entirely at the disposal of the I AM, then we see that here is the needle's eye through which we must pass and beyond which is the possibility of endless development and creative adventure. What matters vitally is that this individual step towards the Life Eternal is taken consciously during our lifetime, for if we wait till after we have left the body, we shall find that we experience mere *continuity* in essentially the same conditions and personality. What a dismal prospect!

Here are a few lines quoted from Edward Carpenter's *Drama of Love and Death*.

> *Limitation and hindrance are part and parcel of the great scheme of the soul's deliverance . . . They stimulate the individualized energy from which for good or ill all our world-activities spring . . . The vast and pervasive soul-stuff of the Universe (in its hidden way omniscient and omnipresent) suffers an obstruction and a limitation, and is condensed into a bodily prison in a point of Space and Time—but with a consequent explosive energy incalculable . . . The Devil—diabolos the slanderer and the sunderer, the principle of division—reigns . . . But this diabolonian process is only a segment of the whole . . . Plunged in matter and the gross body, the human being has learned the lesson of identity and separateness. All the devil can teach him he has faithfully absorbed. Now he has to expand that identity, for ever unique, into ever vaster spheres of activity—to become finally a complete and finished aspect of the One.*

Of course, we can deceive ourselves, and, of course, it is sometimes hard to distinguish between wishful thinking and the true inner voice. This discrimination we have got to learn, often through trial and error. What is of prime importance is the motive. If we genuinely long to serve the Highest, then we may know that the pain of suffering for our blunders will be lifted when the lesson is learned. If the inner motive, consciously or subconsciously, is power for self, then indeed we are heading for ultimate disaster. We may be allowed a long run, since our freedom is always respected, but sooner or later we shall have to face the reckoning and realize the damage we have done to our own soul and to others. The path is undoubtedly full of pitfalls, but it is the way we are called upon to tread. One thing is certain; we must not be daunted by the dangers. All life now is dangerous, for we know all too well that if mankind continues to rush down the slippery slope of materialism, catastrophe will be the result. Therefore, those who have seen something of the spiritual world picture must strive forward to make this inner step. In Christopher Fry's words:

> *Thank God our time is now*
> *When wrong comes up to face us everywhere*
> *Never to leave us till we take*
> *The longest stride of soul man ever took.*
> *Affairs are now soul size,*
> *The enterprise is exploration into God.*

We need to grasp that the point at which ideas bubble into consciousness is for us unique. It is the one point in the universe where we are both an onlooker at a process and at the same time the creator. In every other process, we stand in the position of observer, watching, controlling and experimenting. Here within the mind is something different. We are undeniably the creator of our thoughts, yet at the same time we can observe their coming to birth.

We must accept that we are fully responsible for all we write or speak or create, even if we feel it to be "inspired." We do not transfer this responsibility by saying "it just wrote itself through me." We are channels for the creative source but not mere taps for the water to flow through. The human being, miraculously devised, is that point on earth which can maintain conscious touch with the Source. Thus, he can play a leading part in the redemption of the planet. It has taken aeons of evolution and of suffering for him to reach the point when he can take a step in consciousness and make himself a responsible instrument for working with the Divine Idea. When this step is taken, the pace of his education will leap forward in manifold ways, for he is becoming available for the flow from the oceans of wisdom and creativity.

Thus the finding of the Inner Teacher has immense implications for the future. Each human being has the task of achieving this inner attunement. The provision is wonderfully delicate since in no way does the still small voice encroach upon our freedom. We may begin to practice talking mentally with the Inner Teacher. At first it will seem like a conversation between me and me. But it is offering the opportunity for the Higher Self to impress itself tele-pathically into our consciousness. The crowning beauty of such inner communion is perhaps found in the little book *The Imitation of Christ* in which the fifteenth-century monk Thomas à Kempis sets down his conversations with his Lord. For, let us stress again, the Higher Self is the organ through which we are each personally in direct touch with our Redeemer. The meditative movement known as Contemplative Prayer, presented by Rev. Robert Couson in his book *Into God*, offers a form of training in this contact with the Inner Teacher. We are invited to take as sub-ject for contemplation one of the many biblical sentences spoken by Him who said I AM THAT I AM. The I AM is God, personal-ized through the Cosmic Christ. Thus to speak of Him as the I AM should be acceptable to every creed or belief in an age awak-ening to the Oneness of the human family. Take one of the phrases such as:

Lo I AM with you always, even to the end of the Earth.
I AM come that ye might have life and have it more abundantly.
I AM God: the Holy One in the midst of you.
Be still and know that I AM God.

Let this sound silently in the Mind. In time it will come to be as if the I AM Himself is speaking. Then let it flow into the Heart, and in the third silence, implement this by allowing it to work through the Will. This must inevitably lead over into intercession for the sufferings of the world.

It is indeed a wonder to know that we possess this pearl of great price, this treasure hidden for the finding, this Inner Teacher who is ever present and ready to respond the moment we make the advance to still the busy personality with its strident, anxious thoughts. There is nothing more important in preparation for the difficult years of change which lie ahead.

Mankind comes of age and now has to take full individual responsibility. The emerging spiritual world view implies that God—the I AM working through its instruments—is indeed omnipresent and knows precisely what He is about. This implies that in this present moment we are where He wants us. We may not see quite why we have been given such a difficult situation, but there is nobility in the view that we draw to ourselves the situations necessary for our soul training. Such acceptance is implied in the concept of the Inner Teacher. To act as if this is all true will make us more positive and tolerant human beings.

Clearly, we are concerned with an immensely important inner step, perhaps the most crucial for our time—''The longest stride of soul men ever took.''

For Christ said:

> *Abide in me and I in you. As the branch cannot bear fruit of itself except it abide in the vine, no more can ye, except ye abide in me. I am the vine, ye are the branches. He that abideth in me and I in him, the same bringeth forth much fruit, for without me ye can do nothing.*
>
> *(John 15:4)*

8 | Exploring Inner Space

OUR AGE has indeed achieved miracles in space exploration, but, since all life is made up of paradox and polarity, we recognize that there is a complementary field for exploration of inner space.

To quote Edward Carpenter—the Cosmic I AM speaking:

> There is no peace except when I AM, saith the Lord.
> I alone remain, I do not change.
> As space spreads everywhere and all things move and
>   change within it,
> But it moves not nor changes,
> So I AM the space within the soul, of which the
>   space without
> Is but the similitude or mental image.
> Comest thou to inhabit Me, thou hast the entry
>   to all life—
> Death shall no longer divide thee from those thou lovest.
> I am the sun that shines upon all creatures from within—
> Gazest thou upon Me, thou shalt be filled with joy eternal.
> Learn even now to spread thy wings in that other world.
> To swim in the ocean, my child, of Me and My Love . . .

The stilled center of meditation is the gateway to the infinite. Eliot's phrase, "I said to my soul—be still . . .," indicates clearly that the true I is not the soul, but the directing entity. And we are certainly not our body, that divinely-planned temple into which, as a spiritual being, we can descend to operate in the limitations of earth embodiment.

A little child, aged three, daughter to a friend of mine, declared: "Mummy, I think I'm rather special. I'm the only one of me in the whole world." This shows a dawning realization of identity, a recognition that the little word "I" is unique and only to be applied to oneself—with one supremely important exception. You can say I about yourself. But a Voice within the depth of your mind can say I AM THAT I AM.

We come to know that individuality is something more than separate identity. The word "individual" derives from "individuum," the invisible, the inseparable, "one in substance and essence" (OED).

Another great polarity emerges strongly in our time. The reductionist world view, which sees the whole as essentially a mechanism composed of the assembly of all the parts, stands over against the holistic world picture which sees the whole as a living Oneness from which all the myriad parts are derived and in which they all work and move in harmony and rhythmic interchange.

God thinks. The Universe is a vast continuum of consciousness and creative spirit. Nothing exists that was not first Thought. All is IDEA. All things, including the body and brain, are thoughts of God. Thus, mind is a pulse of the eternal Mind, and whatever is in things can potentially live in our thinking. As spiritual beings, we are all Ideas of God. We might validly reverse Descartes' dictum and say: I AM THEREFORE I THINK.

IDEAS are alive. They must be seen as living beings. The great adepts describe to us the plane of the Archetypes, where the living Ideas can be experienced, thinking themselves experimentally into ever new forms, a realm of seething, creative motion. The forms of nature are the Archetypal Ideas made visible on the material plane.

Medieval scholasticism passionately disputed the issue of Nominalism versus Realism. The latter, going back to Plato, saw Ideals as real. Nominalism, moving on to Aristotelian thinking, contended the ideas were merely the names we gave to things and they have no valid life of their own. Nominalism, in those days, was the progressive school of thought, opening the way to our analytical scientific approach. In our time, the burning issue comes again to the fore. The movement from reductionist thinking to a Holistic world view is the New Realism. Once again we recognize that Ideas are living things.

Here I quote two important passages from Steiner:

> *The scientist contemplates matter as complete in itself, without being aware that he is in the presence of spirit reality, manifesting itself in material form. He does not know that spirit metamorphoses itself into matter, in order to attain to ways of working which are possible only in this metamorphosis. For example, spirit expresses itself through a material brain, in order that man may, by a process of conceptual knowledge, attain to free self-consciousness. By means of the brain, man derives spirit out of matter, but the instrument he uses is itself a creation of the spirit.*

> *If we see in thinking capacity to comprehend more than can be known to the senses, we are forced on to recognize the existence of objects over and above those we experience in sense perception. Such objects are Ideas. In taking possession of the Idea, thinking merges itself into the World Mind. What was working without now works within. Man has become one with the World Being at its highest potency. Such a becoming-realized of the Idea is the true communion of man. Thinking has the same significance for Ideas as the eye for light and the ear for sound. It is an organ of perception.*

Our masculine, intellectual thinking has led us to deny the inner world of spirit, because we can no longer perceive it. We are the observer, a separated entity among separated things. Eddington even called this "the onlooker-consciousness." But true individuation implies achieving conscious reunion with the Oneness of all things. This stepping beyond the position of mere detached observer is indeed possible, and it is a faculty uniting poetic vision with scientific investigation. Our metaphysical poet Thomas Traherne (d. 1674) describes this experience of union in his poem "My Spirit." He possessed the faculty of remembering back into the womb and beyond into pre-existence. In early childhood, he had direct vision of what he called "the true Ideas of all things."

> *My essence was capacity*
> *That felt all things . . .*
> *This made me present everywhere*
> *With whatsoever I saw.*
> *An object, if it were before*
> *My eye, was by Dame Nature's law*
> *Within my soul . . .*

This inner eye is an endless sphere of vision, for it beholds and unites with the eternal Idea in every thing. Thus Traherne describes the inner space we enter in meditation as

> *A strange extended orb of Joy*
> *Proceeding from within*
> *Which did on every side convey*
> *Itself, and being nigh of kin*
> *To God did every way*
> *Dilate itself even in an instant, and*
> *Like an indivisible center stand*
> *At once surrounding all eternity . . .*

> *O wondrous Self: O sphere of light:*
> *O sphere of joy most fair:*

O act, o power infinite:
O subtle and unbounded air:
O living orb of sight:
Thou which within me art, yet me: Thou eye
And temple of His whole infinity:
O what a world art thou, a world within:
All things appear
All objects are
Alive in thee: supersubstantial, rare
Above themselves, and nigh of kin
To those pure things we find
In His great mind
Who made the world.

How clearly this refers to the Ideas within created things. This is pure realism, and it is the essence of the holistic vision and the door to the exploration of inner space. To this adventure there is ultimately no end, for it is the route across the ether frontiers, into higher realms of consciousness, taken by Dante as he climbed the nine terraces towards the Empyrean and the final union in God.

We are called on to awaken the ability to perceive with the inner Eye of the Mind, the All-seeing Eye. This we can all, to some degree, already do. It is the beginning of what Steiner called "sense-free thinking."

Look now at a tree. It matters not whether it is before you or you see it in imagination. There it stands in its strength and beauty. Now "see" its roots beneath the soil. Experience the delicate, sensitive root-tips, where new cells are proliferating what extraordinary intelligence, anchoring themselves to the rock, that the great oak may stand firm against the storm. Allow the storm to strain the boughs and feel the responsive action in the roots. "See" the sap rising beneath the bark. Experience that, in all the nodes and buds, cells again are proliferating and subdividing in a programmed pattern, so that myriad tiny new oak trees burst all over the aged structure. Experience that the tree is truly being sucked up by a force counter to gravity, which draws up the living sap a hundred feet or more. Truly the tree is a point of perfect balance between the primary polarity of gravity and levity. The sensitivity of the Eye of the Mind can, in like manner, enter the rock and feel the gravity weight drawing to the center, and then enter into the candle flame and perceive a force which reaches out to the ultimate periphery and which cannot be touched by gravity. We become the tree, the rock, the flame, by taking possession of the Idea within it, and we are no longer mere observer, for its being is alive within us. In a true sense, we achieve what the Orient has always known and expressed in the great truth—THAT ART THOU.

Francis Thompson speaks of this Oneness achieved:

> *When to the new eyes of thee*
> *All things by immortal power*
> > *Near and far*
> > *Hiddenly*
> > *To each other linkéd are*
> *That thou cans't not stir a flower*
> *Without troubling of a star.*

The All-Seeing Eye can perceive the tree as a structure of etheric light. This is what Wordworth continually knew as a young man.

> *There was a time when meadow, grove and stream,*
> > *The earth and every common sight*
> *To me did seem*
> > *Apparelled in celestial light*
> *The glory and the freshness of a dream.*

For the exploring of inner space, the conception of metamorphosis is essential. Goethe's discovery of the metamorphosis of plants is here of the greatest significance for us. As poet/scientist, he was convinced that there must be a way of approaching Nature not as divided and in pieces but presenting her as working and alive, striving out of the whole into the parts.

In his botanical studies, he arrived at the concept that there is only one basic organ, the leaf, which the forces working within the plant can transform in a great number of ways. The plant first develops the stem-lead, and we do well to take a plant to pieces and set out its leaves in series so as to observe their stages of development. It will achieve the fullness of artistic leaf form at a certain stage, and then the energy will appear to be withdrawn and the leaf to reduce into calyx. Sometimes, it will be very clear that the leaves are set in a spiral and that this virtually spins into the sepals. Then the miracle happens, and the leaf is metamorphosed into colored petal. This secret is often revealed in the tulip when it throws out a "sport" in the form of a petal a centimeter below the corolla. This organ shows as half red petal and half green leaf. Petal is leaf refined from the coarser green into color and scent. We may feel that the plant has indeed reached up and touched the astral world of "free color," an invisible sea of color which reveals itself in the flower. Stamens are seen as petals transformed. This is most notable when a rose is examined and it is seen that the little crinkle or cyst at the top of an outer petal begins, as petals open towards the center, to show pollen and to harden into a central rib. Every organ, including thorns, is metamorphosis of leaf.

Goethe shows that every plant passes through a threefold expansion and contraction, systole and diastole, first in the leaf structure, then in the corolla and finally in the expansion of the fruit with the ultimate contraction into the seed. This is a point of matter returned to formlessness, chaoticized and, therefore, virtually indestructible and capable of receiving the inflow of the *Idea* of the plant when time and conditions are ripe.

Goethe developed a way of looking into the growth of plants

which is both scientific and artistic. He called it "exact sensorial imagination" (Exakte sinnliche Phantasie). It involves the ability to think with accurate imagination through all the stages of the plant's development from seed through flower and back to seed, "recreating an ever-creative Nature," For, in addition to the physical sense of sight, Man possesses also an eye-of-the spirit capable of seeing Ideas. Both, it is true, are part of one integral whole, but there is this essential difference between them: the bodily eye functions automatically, whereas the activity of the spiritual eye depends on the exertion of the will. (See Ernst Lehrs: *Man or Matter,* an important exposition of Goethe's approach to knowledge of Nature.)

Thus Goethe arrived at the conception of the *Urpflanze,* the Archetypal Plant, that invisible but real *Idea.* We must repeat the well-known story of Goethe's first meeting with Schiller as the two men were coming away from a scientific lecture. Schiller expressed his irritation at the dry academic analysis of nature, and Goethe responded with warmth and enthusiasm, pouring out his vision of metamorphosis and his discovery of the "Urpflanze." "But," said Schiller, "that is no experience, that is an idea." "Then," said Goethe, "I am glad to have ideas without knowing it and to see them with my very eyes."

This marks a moment of high importance in the evolution of human thinking when the ability to see and grasp the Idea reawoke in Goethe. With this faculty of inner vision, the New Realism emerged.

There is no aspect of Nature that will not begin to "speak" if we can approach it in this way, allowing the outer senses to play and observe, but at the same time thinking into the hidden Idea which we know to be reflected in the outer form. Then this secret Being will respond within the soul, and this response we can watch for and observe. It is a sort of double-thinking, without and within. And when we recognize the movement of the Idea, we cannot choose but love it, for it is part of us, and we know that the same essential being is present in tree and plant, rock and animal, earth and man. The process is the beginning of inner exploration, and to the understanding of metamorphosis, there can literally be no end. For this approach to Nature, the all-important book is Steiner's *Knowledge of the Higher Worlds: How it is Achieved?* It is a manual for holistic meditation and thinking, for Steiner developed the Goethean vision and techniques and carried it forward into a science of the invisible.

Here, in somewhat lighter vein but with serious intent, I offer a delightful piece of Western Zen. My friend Douglas Harding (author of *On Having No Head*) was struck by the sudden thought—I have no face, no head: If I am honest, I perceive the world around me from a crystal sphere or space, apparently poised on my shoulders. Please look now with a child-like naïveté. (Except ye become as little children, ye shall not enter the Kingdom and the Kingdom is within you.) You see everyone else as having this remarkable eight-inch object upon their shoulders, but you are unique. (There's only one of me in the whole world.) To real experience, you simply have no face: The Zen masters called it your "original face" and laughingly urged you to "cut off your head." Where does this sphere begin or end? Your own shoes, the ground, the trees, the people, the houses, the stars are all contained in it. Instead of "saving face" or "putting a good face on it," you can let your face go and possess the whole world. When we are well, we are totally unaware of the sensory mechanisms of the head. Only when they are ill do we become aware of them as earache or headache. Thus the head, with all its amazingly complex structure, is a focal point to allow a free-ranging spiritual being to be anchored to the material world and operate within it. But once grasp and use the eye of the mind, and the head becomes a crystal sphere in which the Ideas within everything are reflected, as in the Pillar of Mirrors in Gawain's Chateau Merveil, from which he could perceive all that took place in his dominion.

Heraclitus declared that "Everything Flows": modern physics

discovers that solid matter is composed of vortices of energy in perpetual spin at enormous speed. Thus the solidity of this wall or table is pure illusion. Tibetan Buddhism has always known this and teaches the meditator to see solid matter in movement.

For what the senses alone give us is, at first, sheer illusion. Things are not separate, hard and still. All is in movement and the life in each is the One Life. Which, then, is reality—the hard rock that Dr. Johnson kicked to disprove Berkeley, or the spinning vortices? We have physics, mysticism and Oriental wisdom united in the holistic vision.

Enter the world of Inner Space and all is sounding. Everything to the inner ear is giving forth its sound in a great symphony, which is represented by the sacred word and mantra AUM-OM.

> *Look how the floor of heaven*
> *Is thick inlaid with patines of bright gold:*
> *There's not the smallest orb which thou beholdest*
> *But in his motion like an angel sings*
> *Still quiring to the young-eyed cherubins;*
> *Such harmony is in immortal souls,*
> *But while this muddy vesture of decay*
> *Doth grossly close it in, we cannot hear it.*
>
> *(Merchant of Venice)*

The sense mechanisms may be seen essentially as filters which protect us from the power of the Universe. This thought is well expressed in Martin Armstrong's poem, "The Cage:"

> *Man, afraid to be alive*
> *Shuts his soul in senses five*
> *From fields of uncreated light*
> *Into the crystal tower of sight,*
> *And from the roaring songs of space*
> *Into the small flesh-carven place*

Of the ear whose cave impounds
Only small and broken sounds,
And to his narrow sense of touch
From strength that held the stars in clutch,
And from the warm ambrosial spice
Of flowers and fruits of paradise,
Into the frail and fitful power
Of scent and tasting, sweet and sour;
And toiling for a sordid wage
There in his self-created cage
Ah, how safely barred is he
From menace of Eternity.

To this there should rightly be added a couplet implying that our brain-bound, sense-bound thinking protects us from the vastness of Cosmic Thoughts. "Humankind cannot bear very much reality." The exploration of inner space implies that human thought can become one with Divine Creative Thinking. When man merges consciousness with the plane of Living Ideas, there will be a release of human potential such as we can hardly yet conceive. If we can really achieve the balance of the polarity of outer space exploration with the entry into inner space, then a veritable new renaissance must take place.

Such is the destiny of mankind, to take the step in consciousness which implies becoming truly Man. Humanity is born, for as we unite with the world of Divine Idea, we become truly Human Beings, the Tenth Hierarchy, co-creators with God. '

9 | Essene Teachings and Huna Wisdom

IN THE LAST CHAPTER, we spoke of the important step to the finding of the Inner Teacher. This is a major task in human evolution, and we may therefore expect to find that light will be thrown upon it by all expressions of the Eternal Truth.

It would be useful to look at two streams of ancient teaching which appear to hold great truth for our present age, namely the *Essenes* and the *Secret Science of Huna*. These two bodies of knowledge have come to the fore in our generation. With the Essenes, new impetus has been created by the books and translation of Edmond Bordeaux Szekely; for the Huna Code, the discoveries and writings of Max Freedom Long have revived the ancient teachings. These two approaches have so much in common or in parallel that they will illumine our present problem. In both cases, they were guarding what was felt to be the most vital, secret (esoteric) knowledge, which had to be preserved for the future development of the race. What we are discussing is perhaps the core of the evolutionary step which has to be made if mankind is to reach his full potential. Both Huna and the Essenes seem to hold this central truth.

The *Kahunas*, or "Guardians of the Sacred," had inherited their knowledge and skills from very ancient teachings, presumably Atlantean. It was practiced in the Atlas Mountains in the time of Christ, and, indeed, it seems probable that Our Lord knew and taught the Huna wisdom. Max Long has called his last book *The Huna Code in Religions*, showing how the doctrine is found in all the great religions. It was carried through India, under the guidance of the Higher Selves, to a place where it could be preserved in safety—Hawaii. Thus, in no sense must we conclude that it originated as native magic in Polynesia. The Kahunas have now all but died out, and since, like the Druids, they never set anything down in writing, their secret science would have died with them had it not been for Max Freedom Long's remarkable achievement in discovering the secret code hidden like a cypher within the Polynesian language.

Huna demonstrates a form of workable prayer which really achieved results, a "white magic" which constantly brought about instant healing, even to the restoring of crushed and broken bone. Attention was first drawn to the power of the Kahunas through their quite inexplicable ability of "fire walking" unharmed over glowing lava. This should not be written off by our western minds as mere native magic, for, as Long presents it, the Huna knowledge appears to be consonant with our most advanced psychological and spiritual knowledge.

Central to the Huna teaching is the concept of the three selves of man—the Middle Self which is our rational personality, the Low Self or the unconscious, and the High Self. The Low Self is seen not merely as a Freudian sink for all our nasty repressions and perversions but as a being on a more animal stage of development, not rational or intellectual but very intelligent and concerned with serving its Master, the Middle Self. Like a devoted and talented dog, it is immensely willing and if rightly trained and treated is prepared to go to any lengths to help the Middle Self. This surely offers us a very constructive vision of the subconscious and its potential. The Low Self is of course in touch with the Collective Unconscious, the earth memories and the elemental world. This is presumably an explanation of the phenomenon of dowsing. Furthermore, the Low Self is the repository for the life force known as *mana*. This concept is of immense importance. The Low Self can, on demand, produce a surcharge of mana and give it to the Middle Self (this in Huna language is called "Mana-mana"). This can be offered as a gift to the High Self which, receiving it, can convert it into High Mana, a power so strong that it can bring about instant molecular change and do apparent miracles in healing and even in change of circumstances. To understand this, we must grasp the concept of the *aka* body which is essentially identical with the "etheric body" of vital forces known to modern spiritual research. *Aka* is a mysterious spiritual substance linking all beings who have established contact with each other by etheric threads which can stretch indefinitely through space and time. Thus, where we have shaken hands or embraced another, the invisible "*aka* threads" link us with them eternally, if we so wish. Along them, thought clusters can be sent, accounting for what we call telepathy. Healing energy can be projected at the request of the Middle Self. The strongest *aka* cord is between the Low Self and the High Self, establishing a fact of supreme importance for effective prayer, for it implies that the cooperation of the Low Self is essential for our contact with the High Self. Perhaps the lack of this knowledge explains why so many of our prayers are not answered. For the High Self is divine in nature. In Huna language, it is called the *Aumakua*, or "Utterly Trustworthy Parental Being." It is a FATHER-MOTHER Spirit, over-lighting our entire destiny, directing the trials and experiences through which we must pass, watching and guiding us through life on this training ground of Earth. To the Kahuna, it is God, in the sense that it is the one part or facet of the Almighty which we mere humans can really know and contact. They were well aware of higher levels of being, but their primary concern was with workable prayer, and it was enough for them to work with the High Self. In like manner, the Buddha was unconcerned with speculation about God, because he was teaching the Way to Enlightenment.

We must mention the Huna concept of sin. To them, there was no sin but hurting another living thing. If an act hurts nobody, how can it be called a sin? Thus, at one step they were lifted out of the moral codes which have so bedeviled our human relations. In their society, they really lived up to the maxim which all the great religions have laid down in almost the same words: — "Do unto others as you would that they should do unto you." When Captain Cook first discovered Hawaii, he found a society more harmonious and serene than any other in the world, one in which Buddha's doctrine of harmlessness was perfectly respected. The Kahunas recognized that the reason why so many human prayers remain unanswered is that there are blockages in the flow of mana from the Low Self. These are the psychological holdups and complexes which bedevil our progress and must be dissolved if we are to come into true and creative relationship with the Higher Self. They are often caused by some kind of possession in which repressed fear, guilt or hate is really eating at our heart and preventing our taking a truly hurt-free attitude. These were called by the picturesque name of "eating companions." Thus, 2000 years ago the Kahunas knew all about the subconscious, which for us was so recently rediscovered by Freud and Jung, and they knew and worked with the High Self or super-conscious, which is not yet recognized by much orthodox psychology. This extraordinary tradition is therefore in line with our psychosynthesis and transpersonal psychology. The Huna prayers worked and succeeded continually where we so often fail. And this, be it repeated, is not to be seen as native magic from Polynesia but as the last survival of The Secret, treasured by initiates who carried it across the world from Atlantis or beyond and gave it out in teaching and demonstration so that a partial understanding and recollection is found in many religions. They preserved it in the hidden corner of the Pacific, to be rediscovered just in time before the negative, debasing influences of Western culture drove it underground. But now in our reawakening to spiritual understanding, the Secret of the Kahunas, restated in a Western form, seems to hold a pearl of great price, essential for the step in cognition that modern man must take if he is not to perish.

The Essenes inherited their wisdom from Enoch and Moses. Here is a high Zoroastrian impulse, preserved in communities which withdrew from the cities and lived as the "Desert Fathers" near the Dead Sea and as the "Therapeutae" in Egypt. The Brotherhood followed a very strict discipline which by its nature excluded all who were not prepared to accept their severe lifestyle. They were acknowledged to be men of extraordinary religious and moral quality, so healthy and strong that the normal life span was 120 years, so serene and tranquil that all knew they were innerly in communion with the spiritual sources and resonating with the great teachings of the ancient scriptures. The Essenes developed a way of living in conformity with the Divine Law, recognizing that the human being is at every point always in touch with the oceans of Divine Being and that human suffering and distress were the result of willful deviation from the Law on which all natural and cosmic life is founded. Their lifestyle reflected the best of what we now know as Nature Cure or Natural Therapy, organic agriculture and transpersonal psychology, but it was set within a structure of worship and communion which fully recognized the sacredness and unity of all life in Earth and the Cosmos. They sent out their teachers, and it appears that Jesus was the greatest of them. We know from Edgar Cayce's "readings" and other sources that Mary was taken into the protection of the Brotherhood and that Jesus was accepted as their highest initiate, not needing to go through their full training because he knew it all. Indeed, it appears that, in the pattern of human destiny, the Essene order provided a setting in which the impulse of nascent Christianity could be nourished. The movement faded out around A.D. 100 when this function was fulfilled. John the Baptist and John the Beloved were, it appears, also Essene initiates and teachers. It is not, therefore, surprising to find how many Biblical passages are woven into the Dead Sea Scrolls and other Essene documents. This is best illustrated in the splendid book *The Gospel of the Essenes* in which Dr. Edmond Bordeaux Szekely has translated and brought together poetical and scriptural translations from many Essene sources.

They lived by a strict meditative rule based on their Communions with the Angels of the Earthly Mother and the Heavenly Father. These drew their inspiration from Moses' realization that there are great sources of cosmic energy with which we are in touch at every moment and in every part of our Being. These are not mere mechanical forces but are alive, shot through and through with consciousness and being, and working always for the harmonious functioning of all life in conformity with the Divine Law. Thus, they were designated as the Angels, representing the energies we need for vital living so that we can experience true health and harmony of body and soul. These oceans of being are recognized again in the Christian doctrine of the nine Heavenly Hierarchies, from the Cherubim and Seraphim down to the Archangels and the Angels. Steiner, through his spiritual researches, called them Spirits of Form, Spirits of Wisdom, of Love, of Will, of Personality, and so forth. This great vision, of course, equates well with our own Holistic world picture in which we recognize that all life in its infinite diversity of form is yet to be experienced as a great Oneness, a continuum of thought, will and love.

The Essenes practiced seven dawn communions with the Angels of the Earthly Mother which attuned the human being with the Kingdoms of Nature, the living Earth, the trees and the elements. This we must recognize as closely related to the powers of the Lower Self in Huna Lore. It meant that in their rituals of gardening, forestry and farming, in the growing, preparing and eating of food, they were truly calling on the close cooperation of the Lower Self and all its faculties. The Angels of the Heavenly Father, to whom the nightly communions were directed, represent all the qualities of the Aumakua, the realm of the Higher Selves. They began with the affirmation that "The Heavenly Father and I are one" and in succeeding days, resonated with the Oceans of Eternal Life, of Creative Ideas and of Peace. Then they drew on the Cosmic Oceans of Wisdom, Love and Power to vitalize what they called the Thinking Body, the Feeling Body and the Acting

Body. The threefold nature of man, fully known to the Essenes so long ago, is now increasingly recognized in spiritual teaching and advanced psychology: thinking, feeling and willing, working, respectively, through the head or nervous system, the heart or rhythmic system and the metabolic or limb-system.

Then at noon each day, the Essenes practiced their "Contemplation of the Sevenfold Peace." They saw peace or harmony as a dynamic force to which they could attune in body, emotions and mind, in their relations with others and with mankind and ultimately with the Heavenly Father. This brought a tranquility and non-attachment which puts the great Essene teachers on a par with the Kahunas and their doctrine of "No hurt-no sin." It is implied in the Commandment "Love thy neighbor as thyself."

Since it is claimed that Jesus was both an Essene teacher and a Kahuna initiate, and since both doctrines can be reflected in His teachings, it seems valid to think that these two remarkable life-styles, at first sight so different, do in fact spring from the same source and Truth and are, indeed, both guardians of the greatest secret mankind can discover. It must be remembered that we are not merely dealing with an academic study of how the Desert Fathers lived but with a living impulse playing forward into our time and evolving and metamorphosing as it reappears. Indeed, we must feel that many of the great Essenes who cherished the Christ impulse in its early years must be incarnating again at the present time to carry forward the same vital work in a form fitting for this age of the Second Coming.

The Essenes foresaw catastrophe for mankind if deviation from the Law continued. Their Book of Revelations includes passages which are very close to the Apocalypse in the Bible, for this was written by John the Beloved, himself an Essene master. The aim of the communions and the whole lifestyle was to awaken and train enough people to live through a time of calamity and to make centers where the survival techniques and way of living in harmony with the Law could be practiced. If enough men could recover this health and harmony and truly work with the Angelic Forces, then mankind could be saved. The same can surely be said about the need of our own age.

Such, briefly, is the general picture of the Essene lifestyle as presented by Edmond Bordeaux Szekely in his many books. The chief of these published in Britain is *The Gospel of the Essenes,* a poetic and biblical expression which brings together passages we recognize from Scripture and from other ancient sources going back as far as Enoch and the Zend Avesta of Zoroaster. It is a beautiful book and its essential commentary is *The Teachings of the Essenes from Enoch to the Dead Sea Scrolls.* This gives a general description of the Essenes and their teaching, with details of the Communions and the Contemplations of the Sevenfold Peace. These two books are enough to bring the essential approach into our life and meditation. To this Szekely now adds: *The Essene Way—Biogenic Living* (1978), a rewriting of the original book with which he founded the International Biogenic Society fifty years ago. This gives us the practical techniques for a way of living which is directly consonant with all the best of our holistic healing, organic husbandry, natural therapy and what is now called the Alternative Lifestyle.

Let it be stressed that this is not a specific cult or doctrine. His word "biogenic" simply means life-generating. A lifestyle which taps the energies of life through whole and living food and a right relation to nature, earth and heaven and our fellow humans—this is what is desperately needed today. In a true sense, those working in the New Age Movement are Essenes, for almost all aspects are seen to contain some facet of these wide teachings of a way of life which draws upon the Cosmic and Earthly Energies. Thus the Essene Way of Biogenic Living could help many and give more meaning and purpose to what they are already doing. A number of "alternative" centers and enterprises have been founded while still questing to find their real goal and purpose. Perhaps the Essene vision will bring the clarification and inspiration.

But here is an important point. It may be that some historians would challenge Szekely on the ground that his interpretation differs on certain points from what we know of the Desert Fathers. Furthermore, they might say that some of his quotations appear to come from documents unknown to the scholars in the Vatican Library or elsewhere. Realize that we are concerned not with an academic study of a movement 2000 years ago but of an Impulse playing forward into our own time. Such is the stuff of history. The Essene Impulse is born again, flowing afresh into our present situation. Doubtless, it is carried by souls who were alive at the time and come again with the knowledge enriched and metamorphosed to meet the needs of the twentieth century. It is highly likely that Szekely was himself a great Essene, and his living thought is therefore now a pure channel for the Angels of Wisdom to pour their knowledge into modern minds.

The Essenes spent their day in agriculture or gardening, to produce the fruits of the Earth, in meditation, in teaching and also in study of the great works of literature and scripture. This was not, however, mere academic study. They learned the art of resonating with the thought behind the master-work, still alive in the Ocean of Wisdom. In the Sevenfold Peace, we find one contemplation given to "Peace (or Harmony) with Culture." The goal was to come into soul relation with the thinking of the Master expressed in great art and literature. "Moral education is impossible without habitual vision of greatness," to use a phrase of Whitehead's. How much this should apply in our Adult Education!

The Essenes, as we have already said, offered a protective setting for the Christ Impulse at its first entry, 2000 years ago. Is it not likely that the same souls will return again to serve the same impulse at the time of the Second Coming? It is "life generating" indeed, for it is a working with the ever nascent, ever dawning vitality of Him who said "I am the Resurrection and the Life."

It is right, indeed, that survival techniques should be mastered in our age of crisis and that there should be simplifying of lifestyle so that we may learn to work rightly with the living forces of the Earth, without wasteful exploitation of her irreplaceable resources. Unless we achieve this, the human race will destroy itself. Thus, surely what the renewed Essene movement can offer is nothing sectarian, but a way of living which channels the angelic energies of Heaven and Earth and brings life again into line with the Divine Law and the Eternal Ancient Wisdom. It is an aspect of mankind taking full responsibility for its humanity.

Szekely, after a long life, was released in August 1979 into the greater life. Here passed a great initiate. It is certain that that soul will now overlight the wide New Age movement in a significant way. The International Biogenic Society operates in Central America, but it was his great hope that Centers for Biogenic Living should begin to appear in Britain for the teaching of the Essene Way. This could enrich any aspect of the Alternative Lifestyle and the realization of the Holistic Vision.

This chapter shall close with two quotations from the Thanksgiving Psalms of the Dead Sea Scrolls.

> *I thank Thee, Heavenly Father,*
> *because Thou hast put me*
> *at a source of running streams,*
> *at a living spring in a land of drought,*
> *Watering an eternal garden of wonders,*
> *the Tree of Life, mystery of mysteries,*
> *growing everlasting branches for eternal planting*
> *to send their roots into the stream of life*
> *From an eternal source.*
> *And Thou, Heavenly Father*
> *protect their fruits*
> *with the angels of the day*
> *and of the night*
> *and with flames of eternal Light burning every way.*

I have reached the inner vision
and through Thy spirit in me
I have heard Thy wondrous secret.
Through Thy mystic insight
Thou hast caused a spring of knowledge
to well up within me,
a fountain of power,
pouring forth living waters,
a flood of love
and of all-embracing wisdom
like the splendor of eternal Light.

10 | Festivals and Holy Places

WE KNOW our task is to learn to live in the NOW. The present moment is all we have and it contains all our past history. Furthermore, we learn to attune to the Inner Teacher who is our channel of contact with God and the Christ within. With this creative force, each human being can be in touch the whole time. Yet there are certain times in the cycle of the year and certain places on the face of the earth which the wise ones of old knew by actual experience that they could utilize to make closer contact with the Heavenly World through prayer and meditation. Since one of the chief purposes of Earthly existence seems to be to make conscious contact with the Source while one is still embodied, it follows that the Holy Times and Sacred Places have mattered greatly to mankind. In our materialistic age, that contact has been largely lost, and with it, the Festivals have for many become devoid of deeper meaning. But now in a period of spiritual awakening, we recover the living significance of the cycle of yearly Festivals and are also drawn to revive the impulse for pilgrimage to the holy places where direct contact with the Eternal Worlds outside time is still to be achieved by those who know and are sensitive.

The Festivals of the Year can be seen as a great cross, formed by the Solstices and the Equinoxes. The Twelve Holy Nights from December 24 to January 6 are a most magical period in the dark time of the year when days are shortest and Earth has drawn her vital forces into herself. Nature appears to lie in a frozen death-like sleep, but the Being of Earth is then most awake. The Twelve

Holy nights are a time when all is in suspense, as if Earth held its breath, waiting and listening, until permission is granted from the Cosmic Heights for the sap to begin to rise, and the cycle of the turning year begins once more. On December 21, the Sun reaches its most southerly point and begins again to move northward. In three days, it becomes perfectly clear that the days are lengthening, and so December 24 is the time for ritual celebration.

The early followers of Christ celebrated the Christ-Mass on January 6, the Feast of Epiphany and the date of the Baptism in Jordon. In the fourth century, it was moved forward to December 25 to celebrate the Birth of the Baby Jesus. This united the wonder of the Birth with the midwinter solstice. Ancient mystery ritual and the Christian services at midnight of December 24 were united in a great and solemn event. It was called the "seeing of the Sun at midnight," the aim being to develop inner vision so that at the darkest hour the sun could be "seen" through the earth. Thus, the Midnight Hour was, and remains, the most holy moment of contact.

The coming of the shepherds and the beasts to the Holy Babe represents the entry of that impulse of compassion which unites all the kingdoms of nature and the elemental world with the angelic realms. It is interesting that Milton in his *Hymn on the Eve of Christ's Nativity*, actually writes:

> *The shepherds on the lawn*
> *Or ere the point of dawn*
> *Sat simply chatting in a rustic row;*
> *Full little thought they then*
> *That the mighty Pan*
> *Was kindly come to live with them below.*

This is surely a strange hint that Pan is not in fact the cloven-footed devil but the universal Master of the nature spirits and, therefore, in close relation to the descent of the Lord of Light into the body and being of Gaia, the Earth Mother. Alas that our materialistic thinking cuts out the feeling for these great truths. Christmas has degenerated all too often into a festival of pleasure, in which admittedly the flow of compassion and love is shown by our present-giving, our Christmas cards and our festivity. But how often do we pause to think of the slaughter of millions of God's creatures to grace our feasting in honour of the Lord of Love? *Punch* gave us a cartoon showing Oxford Street under its riot of decoration and two ladies looking into Selfridge's window display, in a corner of which a manger and crib had been set up. One lady says to her friend, ''Ah, I see they're bringing religion into Christmas.''

In polar opposition is the Summer Solstice, June 21, when the sunrise achieves its most northerly point. How the heart is moved if we can actually watch sunrise at the winter or summer solstice and even make some annual mark on a wall to catch the first beams of sunlight, so as to prove to ourselves that the great moment has again been reached. Three days later, it becomes undeniably certain that the peak is passed, so June 24, the Feast of St. John the Baptist, is celebrated as Midsummer day. High Summer is the time when Earth has fully breathed out her forces into the cosmos. Clairvoyant vision can see that the structure of the etheric body of the earth is then drawn out by the warmth of the sun towards the cosmic heights. So from time immemorial, men have celebrated Midsummer with rejoicing, with dance and poetry, with music and with bonfires. It can indeed be a time for ''A Midsummer Night's Dream,'' for the elemental world of the nature spirits rejoices. It is true that the fairies dance at this holy time; but, alas, our vision is closed. Midsummer as a religious Festival is largely lost. It will be restored as we recover the vision of the Oneness of all life, when we can in direct experience move out in consciousness into the cosmos with the Earth energies as they are drawn upward to the Sun.

We turn now to Easter, which, as all should know, is a Festival related to the Stars. It falls on the first Sunday after the first Full Moon after the Spring Equinox on March 21st. A movable Easter has its inconvenience for a public holiday, and there have been pressures to fix it, wholly ignoring the fact that on Easter Sunday, intensified cosmic energies flow into the earth. It would be valid here to describe a remarkable experiment made by L. Kolisko, in her scientific work to investigate the etheric formative forces, following indications given by Rudolf Steiner. He showed that it was possible to get an image of the life-force of a plant by making a highly potentized solution of the plant essence through very great dilution and adding a solution of certain minerals which represent planetary forces—Silver Nitrate, Iron Sulphate or Gold Chloride. A piece of litmus paper is placed upright in a saucer with the solution, and the liquid, rising to a certain height, shows the most striking colors and shapes which reveal the invisible etheric forces working in the plant. The technique is known as Capillary Dynamolysis.

In 1943, Easter fell shortly after the equinox on March 28th. The Archbishop ruled that the Easter Full Moon should be considered to be a month later and that the festival should be celebrated on April 25th. The Astronomer Royal maintained that the earlier date was correct. Mrs. Kolisko set out to see what her experiments revealed. Every day she repeated them and a certain pattern showed itself again and again, until on Sunday, March 28th, a resplendent form of shape and color appeared.

On the Archbishop's Sunday in April, there was no difference from the pattern of any other day. As might be expected, a similar strengthening of the etheric forces was revealed on the true Whitsuntide, six weeks later. To the artistic/scientific eye looking at the photographs, there can be no doubt whatever that a remarkable inpouring of spiritual power takes place on the true Easter Sunday. It indicates that Easter is a cosmic event. (see the Monograph "Spirit in Matter" by L. Kolisko)

Easter, that moment in the year when all life is bursting and burgeoning in beauty of flower and frond, was chosen as the time when the greatest event in history took place, and death was re-deemed by Life. Let us use Spenser's splendid sonnet to express this thought.

Most glorious Lord of Lyfe: that on this day
Didst make Thy triumph over death and sin;
And, having harrowed hell, didst bring away
Captivity thence captive, us to win;
This joyous day deare Lord, with Joy begin;
And grant that we, for whom thou diddest dye
Being with Thy deare blood clene washt from sin,
May live forever in felicity!
And that Thy love we weighing worthily,
May likewise love Thee for the same againe;
And for Thy sake, that all lyke deare didst buy,
With love may one another entertayne!
So let us love, deare Love, lyke as we ought,
Love is the lesson which the Lord us taught.

Of course, great Festivals of Easter and its sequel, Whitsuntide, are celebrated finely and traditionally by the Church. For those concerned with the spiritual awakening in the New Age, it will also be celebrated as an inner festival, for it represents the transcending which must take place within the soul. At this time, the soul, buried in the tomb of the body and the senses, may actually reawaken to the reality of spirit within all matter and within itself. Thus Christ is to resurrect in the human heart.

In like manner, Whitsuntide, celebrated by New Age groups as an inner world event, will take on a meaning lost through our materialistic outlook. The Pentecostal coming of the Holy Spirit is not just an event that happened to the disciples so long ago. It is a transformation that can sweep through us all and change us. These great linked Festivals of the Christ Birth, of Death and Resurrection and of the inpouring of the Spirit of God, are revitalized for us in this generation when mankind is becoming Humanity. If it be true that before the end of the century there is to be a transformation of human consciousness, then every Festival will become a time for preparation. Time is running out and the issue is urgent. A wonder approaches and redemption from the results of the Fall becomes possible and even imminent if we awaken ourselves.

The Michaelmas Festival of the Autumn Equinox stands opposite to Easter. We have already spoken of the significance of this as yet unrecognized festival which we are called to celebrate in new ways to represent the community experience of united soul endeavor. Thus, the cycle of the Festivals, as they recur through the year, takes on new meaning as the quickening of the spirit is recognized and experienced. They are not empty forms but moments when the Living Spirit is active, and our lives can be transformed so that we lift out of the entombment in the grave of the earth. They are the moments when the seers of old knew that the heavens were open. "Glory be to God on High and on Earth peace to men of goodwill!"

We begin to feel the close relation of the ancient pagan festivals to the pattern of their Christian successors. It is not simply that the early Christian priesthood found it convenient to take and transform the older rituals but that the Christian Festivals are a true evolution and metamorphosis of the pagan, just as the Mystery of Gologtha fulfills the Ancient Mysteries.

Indeed, we might here quote a saying by St. Augustine: "This which we now call the Christian Religion existed among the ancients, and was from the beginning of the human race until Christ Himself came in the flesh, from which time the already existing true religion began to be styled Christianity."

Thus the Christian Festivals are related to the ancient cycle of the year, since they were originally an expression of the same ageless fount of wisdom.

As we have seen in another chapter, the descent of the Christos was the greatest turning point in history, at which the link between mankind imprisoned in matter and the divine ethereal worlds was established for all time. Esoteric or Cosmic Christianity, as interpreted through the holistic world picture, brings an impulse into human life which fulfills and carries further the knowledge guarded in the Mysteries. This accounts for the surprising readiness of the Druids to accept early Christianity. The Druids were the bearers of the Ancient Wisdom, and their rituals, in a very pure form, were concerned with the establishing of a real flow between the ethereal world of spirit and the life of man. The earth was recognized as a living creature, and the power centers, through which cosmic energy could pour, were known and guarded. The rituals at Summer and Winter Solstices were all concerned with maintaining centers open to celestial influence.

We have inherited beliefs about the Druids based on deliberate slandering of their order by the Roman conquerors, that they might justify their ruthless suppression. It is, for instance, quite untrue that they indulged in human sacrifice. The Druids were the great initiates of their time, establishing Mystery Centers for learning and teaching of the civilized arts. Their religious wisdom and tradition was passed on largely by word of mouth, and, therefore, little survived by way of record when the order was given for them to disperse. Thus, they simply faded away into their forests, like mist before the morning sun. Their influence was replaced by the much coarser predatory system which the Roman conquerors established. We may feel that the Druids were nobly carrying forward the stream of most ancient wisdom which went far back, doubtless to Atlantis. Their practices were an example of an advanced form of real stewardship of Mother Earth, maintaining, as did the Essenes, the communions with the oceans of angelic life and power. This involved most conscious use of those moments in time when contact was fully open to the Divine Worlds (the Festivals) and those sacred points on the earth's surface through which the etheric energies could flow (the power points and light centers). They were preservers of the great energy grid which related spirit within Earth to Spirit in the higher eternal planes. Thus, the Druids at once recognized the esoteric truth of Christianity. Indeed, when the first news of the descent of the Christ, his Death and Resurrection, was carried to the Celtic West, the Druid masters were already expecting it, since they had clairvoyantly seen the aura of the earth changing and becoming filled with a new light. Thus they knew that somewhere the supreme event for which they had been waiting had at last happened and that the Exalted Lord of Light had descended into the life forces of the Earth. So their work was done and they could merge with the Christian stream. The high culture of Celtic Britain arose from this merging of Druidism and its mystery centers with the esoteric Christian Stream which expressed itself through the Celtic or "Culdee" church and the founding of the early monasteries.

Holy Times and Sacred Places! We learn now that there is a network of Power and Light Centers across Britain and, indeed, spanning the World. As the body has its chakras and acupuncture points, so with the body of the Earth. All is Energy. The oceans of Life and Will and Thought, flowing in subtler vibrations, animate and sustain the living organism of the planet. Light Invisible flows through the Universe, and our Earth, circling to eternity, is integrated into the vast pattern of movement.

Listen innerly:

> *There's not the smallest orb which thou beholdest*
> *But in his motion like an angel sings,*
> *Still quiring to the young eyed cherubins.*

All natural forms emit their sound and the whole is expressed in the sacred Word OM or AUM. Countrymen of old sometimes claimed that they could hear the corn growing. This should not, however, be interpreted as physical hearing but as the inner ear, in supersensible attunement. Our distant forebears, led by advanced spiritual beings, were sensitive to these holy points on Earth's Surface where the flow of Light Energy was strongest. Here one could lift the soul in prayer and invocation and know the reality of God.

In her book *The Light in Britain*, Grace Cooke, as a very advanced sensitive and clairvoyant, describes a tour she made of the ancient centers like Stonehenge and Avebury. Here she re-experienced in inner vision that they were great temples for allowing the inpouring and storing of spiritual Light.

We have learned of the remarkable system of ley-lines which cover our land with an intricate network. Alfred Watkins first discovered this phenomenon and wrote the book *The Old Straight Track* (1927). The leys appeared to be sited trackways, absolutely straight and marked by standing stones, tumps, stone circles, cairns and beacons, with Christian churches frequently sited on the crossing points of the leys. He admitted that he could get no adequate explanation of their real purpose. In our generation, the knowledge has arisen of the flow of earth energies, as presented by such writers as John Michel and T. C. Lethbridge. We have understood ever more clearly that matter and form are derived from cosmic energy and creative idea. Thus it looks as if the supposed "trackways" may compare with our pylon lines for carrying energy across the country from the spiritual generating plants. A race of men who knew of the earth force and could handle it established this structure of ley lines centered upon the great temples. Thus was established the grid or network of light and power centers.

When churches are sited upon such centers, the flow of the Earth energies, as traced by dowsers, often takes a most positive course around the altars and beneath the domes. It flows like water or the bloodstream and, therefore, can obviously be influenced and channelled to some degree by human thought and intention. The makers of the leys were working with the living body of the Earth. The standing stones compare with the needles used by Chinese acupuncturists. (Read *Needles of Stone* by the dowser Tom Graves.) The dowser can demonstrate with pendulum and rods that a wide field of energy surrounds many of the standing stones and that they have their etheric field and their chakras, often comparable to those in the human body.

Now we must consider the significance of pilgrimage, for the pilgrim ways often run along the old trackways. Admittedly, the overt purpose of the medieval pilgrimage was usually focused upon the relics of some saint, and this usually proved very profitable for the establishment concerned. Yet we have seen that the cathedrals are often built on power points which themselves are sites of ancient temples. Thus, when the throng of pilgrims gathered in devotion and prayer, the healing forces flowed. Conceive what power must have been generated by the endless streams of pilgrims to Compostella, Canterbury, Rosslyn Chapel or Chartres. In the age of faith, the motive and the prayer would have activated a continuous flow of Divine energy and "miracles" of healing would not infrequently have occurred.

In our day, thousands, indeed millions, of people come as tourists to these architectural centers, and problems of preservation sometimes arise when so many feet come walking through. Imagine what could be achieved for the redemption of our benighted planet if the motive of mere tourism, however worthwhile and enlightened, were converted once more into pilgrimage. There is great need for the revival of the pilgrimage impulse, and this becomes possible through the spread of spiritual knowledge and understanding. We spoke of this concerning the centers dedicated to the Archangel Michael. We now know that Michael represents a living force of Cosmic Being, and that this should be invoked. We know that the Michaelic Beings are present invisibly in these centers. Every holy center has its guardian. We should never enter church or sanctuary or holy place without offering up a prayer of invocation to the guardian, giving him thanks when we depart. Such a deed of recognition and love for the invisible Presence assuredly evokes a response. Furthermore, our ritual gestures, offered in good faith, call forth an answer on higher planes, since the angelic worlds are in close telepathic contact. Thus, on our pilgrimage visit we should, so far as circumstances allow, circumambulate the building in processional movement, if possible carrying candles. Music, poetry and invocation will intensify the dedicated prayer. We may be sure that our little lights will meet a response from ethereal Light, along with our music and incantation from celestial harmony and the sounding of the WORD. The ritual, of course, culminates in prayer and invocation and may well end in joyful dance. Each pilgrimage may be freshly created to suit the circumstance (using discretion to avoid negative reactions from tourists!)

This is the age when Michael does battle with the Beast. The powers of darkness, Ahrimanic and Luciferic, have no compunction about taking possession of body, soul and intellect. But the angelic powers of Light may not and will not do so. Respecting human freedom, they call for our conscious and willing cooperation and invitation. Does this not imply that our New Age Movement is called upon to learn to activate the grid of sacred centers? What power could be channeled if this could be rightly achieved! Each time we visit a church or a cathedral, we can by inner attitude turn it into pilgrimage and thus do something to strengthen the Power of the Light.

Use now the eye of Imagination. Rise up in consciousness and look down upon our Island. See the Light Centers glimmering— Stonehenge, Avebury, Glastonbury, Iona, St. Michael's Mount, Westminster Abbey, Durham and all the Cathedrals of Britain, the monasteries, noble ruins which have for centuries been impregnated with prayer and meditation, the Christian Churches great and small where ley lines cross, the healing centers, the New Age communities and centers for organic husbandry, the dedicated amber lights of the Lamplighter Movement (see Appendix II)—and on and on the list could be extended, till the country is covered with glimmering points of light. See the lines of force criss-crossing and unifying in an immense network or grid. And note again how the ancient Druidical pattern is overlayed by the Christian. The spiritual light and Earth-power stored at the ancient temples like Stonehenge and Glastonbury is indeed there and waiting for release. And the Holy Mountains are veritable storehouses of spiritual power guarded by angelic Beings and waiting to be tapped and used in the service of Michael. These are a precious heritage, for they could be misused. We may look down and with inner vision link St. Michael's Mount, Skirrid, Wrekin, the Eildon Hills, Glastonbury Tor, Malvern, Tryfaen, Schiehallion. There are many more and new ones to find and, through suitable pilgrimage, to activate.

We have compared this network to a great electric grid. If, metaphorically, the cosmic switch were thrown, light and power would instantly flood throughout the land. Imagine that, as you watch, this happens. Even give it a countdown—five, four, three, two, one, NOW! Suddenly Britain comes alight. Are we ready for such an event? Is the grid sufficiently strong and united to take the inflooding charge of the Light? Are all its links established?

The angelic forces could use all our power points and light centers, if we can but do our essential task of preparation. What is needed is a veritable structure of prayer, invocation, pilgrimage, and conscious linking by projected thought. Those who on this plane are actually guardians of these Holy Places have a special responsibility and need our active support, as do the invisible angelic beings who overlight the sacred centers.

It will, of course, need imaginative cooperation and courage to put this general project into effect, but there are many indications that the activating of the Network of Light Centers is an imperative requirement from the higher sources and that it is part of the Plan. LET LIGHT AND LOVE AND POWER RESTORE THE PLAN ON EARTH.

Truly in Britain this endeavor must involve Arthur. For Arthur, the Champion of Albion, is to be seen as the great Commander of the British Folk-Soul, the principle of true royalty, justice and chivalry, part of the chain of High Command under Michael and the Christ. Legend has it that the "Once and Future King" sleeps with his Knights within the hollow hill, waiting for the moment when Christian Britain is in dire need and sends forth the call. Then he comes forth to do battle for the Light. It may be that the moment for the Return of Arthur is approaching. The symbol may be taken as referring to a power sleeping within the collective unconscious of the race, which will be aroused from its slumber by the great challenge. This has been experienced before and will be again. We may also link it with the spiritual power stored in the Holy Mountains which can be drawn upon by right attunement.

As we approach the crisis of change in the next decades when so much of the old must be swept away to make way for the coming of the New Dawn, then surely a major human task is given us. We must first recognize the Festivals of the year as times when the Spirit can powerfully flow, and we must learn to celebrate them with a new understanding of their Cosmic Significance. Christmas and Epiphany, Easter and Whitsuntide, St. John's and Michaelmas will take on new meaning as moments for deep spiritual experience and union. Then we must unite the Festivals of Time with the Centers of Light and Power, those "intersection points of the timeless with time." It is a question of enhanced consciousness. Even though our efforts are modest, they are part of the immense "Operation Redemption."

O Light Invisible, we give thee thanks for thy great glory.

11 | Man's Relation to the Animal Kingdom

THE INTENTION OF THIS BOOK has been to take the "holistic" world picture, which sees the Whole as Holy, and apply it to different facets of our living. Obviously "Oneness" means what it says. Everything works as a stupendous unity, the smallest part in harmonious relation to the whole. All is interconnected in an intricate pattern of enormous complexity, yet always working as one. New light will be thrown on anything if we can learn to look at it "holistically." So it is with our relation to the animal kingdom, an issue which has the profoundest significance for human destiny.

I remind you that none of these ideas are dogma which you are expected to believe. But learn to hold them in thought and reserve judgment, watching whether they enrich your view of life and have the ring of truth.

WHAT, THEN, ARE THE ANIMALS? Take a big leap in thought. All manifestation in form derives from Divine Creative Thought. God, the Source, thinks everything into being.

FIRST COMES CREATIVE IDEA. The Thinking will first create the *Archetypal Ideas*, strands within the Ocean of Thought, which in due course will manifest in form.

These great spiritual truths can be apprehended by the intuitive faculties which have atrophied or gone dormant in so many people. But they are awake in the poets and, therefore, certain great poems can be used to open our understanding. So let us listen afresh to Blake's splendid poem, *The Tyger*.

Tyger! Tyger! burning bright
In the forests of the night,
What immortal hand or eye
Could frame thy fearful symmetry?

In what distant deeps or skies
Burnt the fire of thine eyes?
On what wings dare he aspire?
What the hand dare seize the fire?

And what shoulder and what art
Could twist the sinews of thy heart?
And when thy heart began to beat?
What dread hand? and what dread feet?

What the hammer? What the chain?
In what furnace was thy brain?
What the anvil? What dread grasp
Dare its deadly terrors clasp?

When the stars threw down their spears,
And watered heaven with their tears,
Did he smile his work to see?
Did he who made the Lamb make thee?

Tyger! Tyger! burning bright
In the forests of the night
What immortal hand or eye
Dare frame they fearful symmetry?

Now look again at the first chapter in Genesis. God creates heaven and earth "without form and void." He creates the fishes and birds "after their kind" and then all the animals "after their kind" and the plants and trees "after their kind." And Man— "male and female created he them, after His own image." "Thus the heavens and the earth were finished and all the host of them."

But in Chapter 2 v. 5, we are told that "God made every plant of the field before it grew for he had not yet caused it to rain upon the earth."

And in v. 5, "God formed man of the dust of the ground and breathed into his nostrils the breath of life, and man became a living soul." Then Eve, from his fifth rib, as a help-meet.

Thus it describes *two creations*, the first being the archetypal Ideas of plants and animals. This is what is implied by the phrase "after their kind." Only later are these living Ideas realized in visible form.

This is born out in spiritual research. There is indeed a realm of the archetypes of each species. We come to the concept of what Goethe called the *Type*, the spiritual being who can be called the *group Ego* of animal or plant species. The fundamental difference between man and animal is that in man the individual ego descends into embodiment, but in the animal it remains on the etheric plane, controlling all members of the species through its thinking, which operates in what we call *instinct*. Thus man has individual reasoning and choice, which is impossible for the animals.

We may think of a great family of the group egos overlighting and directing animal life. Each human ego is unique, something comparable with a species or type. The plants also have a group ego, an angelic being to be found on the astral plane. Therefore, the plant is physically less conscious than the animal, since its ego does not descend close to the earth vibration. The whole of evolution is a drive towards ever greater consciousness. As Teilhard de Chardin has shown, there is a built-in impulse within the cell toward "complexity" into ever more elaborate organization, each step in greater complexification resulting in higher consciousness. From this he concludes there must be a plan. It cannot be fortuitous.

The entire majestic operation is in order that consciousness and ever more refined consciousness should be developed. "Being" takes on embodiment and passes through its relevant phase of earth experience, to be released again when its "body" has done its service and is discarded. This body then returns to the elements from which it was formed, and the spirit to its source, to plunge again into form when time is ripe. Metamorphosis, transformation, is the method of working. All "dying" is the necessary process of releasing the essence from the drastic limitations of embodiment.

Thus, the animal world is perpetually lifting towards ever greater individuation, so the fragments of the group-ego may approach the human experience. Surely this implies that the most advanced members of the animal species are developing soul quality and intelligence which will enable them in due course to incarnate in a simpler form of human body. We all know dogs and horses which are showing a quality of intelligence and personality approaching the human. They are pulling out of the group-ego. Our love and training of them is doing something to lift and redeem the animal kingdom. Be sure that the Pythagorean concept of metempsychosis is not valid—the belief that the human ego can reincarnate as an animal or, in Malvolio's phrase, "that the soul of thy granddam might haply inhabit a bird."

But it certainly appears that animals can "individuate" and take the onward step towards human consciousness as an individualized entity able to step beyond instinct, and so perhaps become able to take on human embodiment in a later incarnation.

Max Freedom Long, researching into the Huna secret, suggests that perhaps the advanced animals progress to the status of the human Low Self, and that the Middle Self may in due time move up to being a High Self.

Perhaps the concept of the group-egos of the animal species helps to make it clear that the animals are indeed ensouled creatures, though not yet in the sense of the human soul, immortal and personally responsible through rational intelligence. We know that there is a mass of evidence from psychic sources of the survival after death of outstanding animals who, through human love and care, have reached a stage approaching individuality. The lesser animals below the primates, as an expression of the group being, are creatures of sensitivity and feeling, but on death they will merge again with the soul-pool of their species, since they will not have advanced far enough to individuate.

We should recognize the significance of the many examples in recent years of an ever closer relationship between men and wild animals; for example, *Elsa the Lion,* or Len Howard's *Birds as Individuals,* or Conrad Lorenz's experience described in *King Solomon's Ring.* It appears that ever more frequently the barriers of timidity between individual animals and men are being broken through, and then a fascinating new contact becomes possible, and a new study of animal nature opens up.

The experiences with otters and dolphins are wonderful to a degree, suggesting how warm and loving a contact is possible between men and the animals. The dolphin is so great a mystery—brain power as great as man's and a desire to protect and help humans whenever opportunity arises, as if they are a species of almost angelic beings who have opted to take on animal form in service of mankind. Think, then, of the horrible implications of the plan which men have devised of training these wonderful creatures to act as living torpedoes to destroy enemy vessels! This is an example of the perversion of human thinking and of blind ignorance and insensitivity. That splendid book *Kinship With All Life* by Boone reveals the amazing telepathic powers of a wonderful dog. Such relationship will open up a world of consciousness beyond our own, for the animal is in telepathic contact with the mysterious being of Mother Earth.

The whole of evolution is a lifting up of the levels of consciousness. Teilhard sees the ever-continuing process of complexification, leading human souls to come together in trans-personal groupings which will open up to cosmic consciousness and God-consciousness in ever greater creativity and he writes: "We have glimpsed the marvels of a common soul."

But beware: the debased human being will not reincarnate as an animal. He has developed beyond that. But he may descend into a new bestiality far below the beautiful realm of animal instinct. It appears that in our time, human beings are appearing with acutely developed intellect and powerful will and ego drive, but with no heart to hold the balance. These are the horrible creatures who can torture their fellow men in concentration camps or the animals in the vivisection laboratory. Here we sense a soul drive towards coarsening of human feeling and destruction of tenderness, brutalizing the human species.

So let us return to the concept of Oneness and acknowledge now that such use of will and intelligence for cruelty is dragging down the whole human race. We are one family—MANKIND—derived from the great Divine Source. The noosphere, the layer of human consciousness, is integrally part of the thinking of the living organism of Earth. We are each part of the whole and are all tarnished by the dark impulses which flow through our world. In a deeper sense, CRUELTY IS INDIVISIBLE. We condone it by passive acceptance. (This thought is well developed by Jon Wynne-Tyson in his fine book *The Civilized Alternative*.)

Thus mankind is loading upon itself a karmic debt of enormous weight and proportions by its collective treatment of the animal kingdom. Much of this cruelty, as in the blood sports, may be due to sheer lack of thought or rudimentary imagination. We all share the responsibility and the degrading effects of cruelty. Ours is a violent society in which greed and desire lead to rivalry, hate, fear and finally war as an accepted way of gaining our ends. The constant stressing of violence and cruelty by the media impregnates it ever deeper into the human psyche. The redemption of mankind turns on individual and collective acceptance of an impulse to greater compassion, a "gentling" of human nature. And this impulse is very apparent in our generation and, it may be, brings with it a power which can transform and cleanse our world.

In deeper soul experiences, we are one with the essential being within all nature, for the One God is present as the essence within each and all. Thus, with this awakening and quickening of the spirit comes inevitably a striving for the great Buddhist goal of harmlessness.

The ancient "Huna" wisdom, we have seen, taught that "where there is no hurt there is no sin." A quality of personality develops which is not prepared to hurt. In due course, this becomes an inability to hurt by deed or word,for the mystic knows the truth of the Oriental aphorism: THAT ART THOU. The essential core of all the great religions is the doctrine DO UNTO OTHERS AS YOU WOULD HAVE THEM DO UNTO YOU. In the integrative view of life, we learn to know that we cannot hurt others without, in the long run, bringing retribution on ourselves. But, having lost the Oneness Vision, we have developed such an aggressive, masculine attitude that we allow ourselves to exploit the kingdoms of nature recklessly to our own advantage, not realizing the price we shall have to pay.

So in this light, we must consider the practice of vivisection, that terrible blot on our modern civilized world. To justify vivisection by the argument that animals do not feel is sheer hypocrisy. Those who say so are simply revealing themselves as insensitive or brutalized, lacking in common sense or normal feeling. One of the terrible human results of animal research is that the young medical student, often filled with horror and disgust at first seeing and carrying out live experiments in vivisection, becomes used to it and even indifferent to the suffering caused. This is a lowering of our standard of humanity. Let us face it that we are all involved in the soul-degradation (degrading, dragging down) that is implicit in vivisection, blood sports, bull-fighting, factory farming and the conditions in many slaughter houses. Animal experiment undoubtedly allows sadistic tendencies to rise.

This is not to say that all experimenters are sadists or that no experiments are of value to mankind. It is saying that the practice of vivisection is debasing to man and that an enormous number of experiments are repetitive and valueless and could be dropped. This has frequently been admitted. The fact that well over five million live animals were sacrificed in this country alone last year, 80 percent of them without any anaesthetic, many of them in conditions of excruciating pain and misery, should be enough to wake us up to what is happening. If we eat chicken, we are condoning the batteries. If we eat veal, we should know and innerly experience what it means to the calf to spend its whole life in a narrow pen in semi-darkness, unable to move or turn about or lie down. If we have once seen pictures of force-feeding of geese in France to manufacture pâté de fois gras, we shall never eat that "delicacy" again. Anyone who uses sealskin should know of the brutal clubbing to death of baby seals.

It is right that public feeling should be aroused in protest. Not until the films of Auschwitz and Belsen were released did the tide of horror rise in public opinion. We had known of the camps years before, but not until emotion was touched did the public conscience rise. If films about factory farming and some of the animal experiment centers could be released, there would be a surge of protest. For what is happening in the vivisection laboratories is comparable with what happened in the concentration camps. The same terrible indifference to the sufferings of the Jews is now meted out on the helpless animals. The logical end of vivisection may also be experiments on humans. But people are too indifferent, unimaginative and ignorant, and the profit motive of financial gain in the farming industry and the pharmaceutical industry is so all-powerful in our present society. Therefore, only slowly does the tide of protest rise—but it is rising.

All are called on to wake up and make themselves aware of what is happening. Indifference is impossible if once we realize what is being tolerated by authority in the name of science. Read *Slaughter of the Innocents* by Hans Ruesch. This is avowedly an impassioned statement, though based on some years of research into the methods used in animal research laboratories. Ruesch intends to arouse our feelings and he succeeds, and the book makes grim reading. The whole problem is complex, and total abolition of animal experiments is a goal to be achieved by stages. But as slavery and child labor were abolished through public pressure and political action, so will vivisection be. It is a blight on our civilization, a canker which degrades mankind, as are also the methods used in factory farming.

Our concern is with the arousing of compassion, an overcoming of the taboo on tenderness which has so hardened and blunted our feelings in the last generations. For how long has our society been concerned with the martial virtues, the so-called "glory" of war, the playing on the instincts of aggression, the acceptance of cruelty as a valid way of gaining ends! How much does all this violate the essential tenderness of the human soul in its love for life! Here are two trends in balance, and the task of becoming human is gradually to transmute the brutalizing and violent impulses.

To quote John Galsworthy:

> *Nothing so endangers the fineness of the human heart as the possession of power over others; nothing so corrodes it as the callous and cruel exercise of that power; and the more helpless the creature over whom the power is cruelly and callously exercised, the more the human heart is corroded. It is the recognition of this truth which has brought the conscience of our age, and with it the law, to say that we cannot any longer with impunity regard ourselves as licensed torturers of the rest of creation; that we cannot for our own sakes afford it.*

And Schopenhauer:

> *The unpardonable forgetfulness in which the lower animals have hitherto been left by the moralists of Europe is well known. It is pretended that the beasts have no rights. They persuade themselves that our conduct in regard to them has nothing to do with morals or that we have no duties towards the animals; a doctrine revolting, gross and barbarous.*

Now apply the touchstone of the wholeness viewpoint. The oneness surges into our consciousness. Compassion, a new tenderness and sensitivity, a more feminine protectiveness to all life, seeps into and through our society wherever it can find channels of entry. Something is indeed happening. So while violence at one level is on the increase, for more and more people the practice of cruelty is becoming impossible. The movements concerned with animal welfare are symptoms of the beginnings of a profound change. The new society which is coming to birth will be composed of people who will no longer be ready or able to inflict the barbarities of cruelty now being practiced. Factory farming and vivisection will in time become unthinkable and will drop away. So also will it be seen that the taking of life for sport or in warfare is no longer to be tolerated. We are still a long way from achieving this, but those who labor for the new sensitivity are taking part in a great awakening to man's true relation to kingdoms of nature, and this understanding comes from the sense of the Spirit of Earth as a living creature, our Mother Earth of which we are part.

Now let us once more stretch our minds in a flight of imagination. What does it mean: "God made man after his own image"? Not, surely, that God is an old man with a long beard somewhere up in the sky! God is invisible, ubiquitous, everywhere, always, a great Being of Spirit, Thought, Love and Will. A lesser being "after his image" will also be spiritual, invisible, universal, capable of moving anywhere, focusing thinking and willing and feeling. Such is the *real* "I" of man. *This* is what we really are in essence. God *first* made the human archetype. From the beginning of Creation, the Idea of Man if formed, the great Potential that through long evolution will be realized in physical form. Thus, the body gives the physical basis for thought, feeling and will. It takes long evolution to produce the vehicle through which a divine spiritual being, the I, the Essence, the human archetype, can operate in the drastic limitation of substance and earth vibration.

Last to appear in physical evolution, Man is first in Idea. "Male/ female created He them," beings of balance and rhythm, creative masculine and sensitive, life-cherishing, feminine in harmony. This invisible, yet unbodied, Being, an attribute of God, moved among the archetypal Ideas of plants and animals as one who is a symphony of all creation.

Creative evolution is the process of realizing this archetypal Idea of Man. Divine thought pours across the ether frontiers to shape Ideas into visible form. Always and from the first this invisible being stands centrally, like unto the Image of God. All the lesser archetypal ideas are contained within it.

Can we see, imaginatively, that the animal kingdom and all its species are in fact facets and attributes of the Whole Idea of Man, specialized and put forth in form before the Body of Man is ready to appear?

This approach was first given by Rudolf Steiner through his researches into the spiritual worlds in his books *Man as Symphony of the Creative Word* and *Occult Science*. It is scientifically developed by H. Poppelbaum in *Man and Animal* and *A New Zoology*. Though on first hearing the ideas may seem surprising, they do, I believe, give us the real key to our present subject.

Man in embodiment is what he is because he has held back long enough to reach a perfection fairly close to the archetype. Facets of the whole have chosen to specialize earlier and manifest their functions in physical form. These are the animals. Thus the ruminants may be seen as the digestive system externalized. Across the face of the earth is extended this mechanism of digestion, the cow consuming grass and manuring the living earth. The lion seems to be the chest in specialized development, the rhythmic system of heart and lungs. How slight are its digestive organs, how powerful its maned shoulders and thorax, how royal its glance and its roar! The eagle, representing the bird kingdom, is seen as a metamorphosis of head and larynx. It has no great intestine, its body is a system of warm air sacks to keep it floating, the glory of its plumage flashing in the sun compares with the flashing of thoughts in man.

Here are the beasts of the Evangelists, bull, lion and eagle, the fourth being Angel Man, the Archetypal Idea. The clue is that every animal species is a part of the body externalized and specialized before the central Being of Man is fully embodied. Marvelous tools are made of hand or foot or mouth, through unbalanced and specific development of some part of the whole. Man has held back. The hand is truly a baby embryonic organ, not a tool like the talon; it can therefore be used to handle all tools or to play the Kreutzer Sonata. The arm itself, lifted out of the gravity field, can be used in acting or ballet for expression of soul and emotion. The key to the new zoology is to find the human organ which is the counterpart of the animal species. Thus snakes are the guts. The fishes, as recognized in astrology, are the feet.

The crustacea, floating in the sea, are like the floating organs in the blood such as kidneys, and it is well known that blood and sea water are chemically practically identical. Thus man, the microcosm, reflects the macrocosm, and the bodily organs appear spread out through the animal kingdom.

Hold this idea that your body is a symphony of the animal species. You as Man are lifted into the vertical stance, your leg driving straight down to the gravity center of the earth, your head poised on the upright spine and open like a chalice to the inpouring of spiritual thought. The horizontal spine of the animal means that the head is never freed from gravity and is used as a major tool, while the leg, even in the galloping horse or jaguar can never be fully straightened or given over to gravity. Thus, upright Man is the perfect meeting point of two worlds, the ethereal and the physical, the eternal and the temporal.

Man is the symphony of the created world.

See, then, that man did not evolve out of the ape. Rather should we see the ape as a tragedy who just failed to "hold it" till he became man, who specialized in function and externalized himself just a little too soon. The baby chimpanzee has its head poised like a man's, with a fine frontal lobe and well-shaped face, though it is already lined like an old man. But as the days pass, you can see him fall back into an ape, with receding brow, protruding jaw and bent stature, dragged down by gravity. As Steiner has pointed out, you can think from man down into ape; you cannot really think ape up into man—proof enough that the primates represent a failure to reach up to the archetypal pattern. We have to include the descent of a spiritual being in our concept of evolution. This being was never animal, but it works upon the sheath of the body to lift it ever near its perfection of Idea.

Now we see something of our true relation to the animal kingdom. Grasp imaginatively this holistic concept. All animals are truly our greater body, and we are related to them all and their secrets are in us. This may be thought through on the soul level. In order to become truly human, we have to eject the animal nature from our soul. The hyena in us, the wolf, the snake, the fox, needs to be sublimated and transmuted. As man, we need to rise above these qualities, which in their rightful place are noble and useful, but when manifesting in the human ego can be despicable. Scavenger hyena is an essential part of nature's pattern, but he is not fitting if manifesting as a human faculty.

Thus, we may see we have risen to Manhood on the sacrifice of the animals. We are the crown of creation, the summit of the pyramid, but we owe an infinite debt to the animal kingdom that we have attained this point in evolution. The holistic vision of Man and life must recognize that the unitary working of nature is built on the sacrifice of the lower species, giving itself for the nourishment of the higher. It is not so much "red in tooth and claw" as a pattern of mutual aid and ritual sacrifice. Think of that glorious bird, the gannet, plunging from a height to spear the flashing mackerel twenty feet below the surface of the sea. Gannet is streamlined for this function and he is beautiful. Gannet/mackerel are one. Group Ego Gannet and Group Ego Mackerel are closely linked in nature's spiritual family. So, it is throughout nature.

No animal (except man) kills for pleasure or takes more than it needs. The fed lion moves hurtlessly among the antelope, hunting only when needing food and then culling the weakest member of the herd.

If such a picture should sound somewhat fantastic, realize that it is, as an imagination, portraying the truth behind the Zodiac, that ancient symbol of soul evolution which emerged in essentially the same form in every culture, and in our time is becoming central to the new psychology. There, again, are the four beasts of the Evangelists as the great cross of the Zodiac—Taurus, the bull, as Mother Earth receiving the inpouring of the cosmic energies of the Ram; Leo, the royal lion, representing individuation, the assertion of the ego which can become a warrior for God; Scorpio, the death-dealing impulse which can transmute itself into the soaring eagle, in order that Aquarius, the Angel Man, may pour out the spiritual waters of the New Age. The Zodiac is called the Animal Circle and presents man—each one of us—as a spiritual being, achieving true humanity through relating rightly in balance (Libra) with all the energies of Earth and Heaven, that Mary, the Virgin within the soul, may dedicate herself in service to the Master and Lord whose symbol is Pisces, the Fishes.

So it is in that mysterious colorful art of heraldry, representing the achievement of the knightly soul, that it may deserve the accolade from its king. There is a regular zoo of heraldic beasts representing animal qualities and energies to be sublimated and controlled by the soul. The shield, representing the aspiring personality, has two supporters, our spiritual guides. These are often fabulous beasts, like the unicorn or pegasus or stag, which take their place in supporting the evolution to true Manhood. The goal is to become *human*, from the Egyptian word *hu*, meaning the enlightened one, the fulfilled being, and in this lies our true relation to the animal kingdom.

All nature fulfills itself in sacrifice and mutual aid, but man, steward of the planet with dominion over all, has failed in his stewardship and deviates from the Law. He pollutes the planet, uses up its resources in reckless extravagance to satisfy his desires, exploits the animals, hunts and kills them for pleasure, tortures them by vivisection in the name of science and forces the rhythms of nature in factory farming.

To think ourselves into this holistic world view touches the imagination and awakens dormant faculties of perception. It can lead to something of a breakthrough into a new empathy with nature. If we can develop what Coleridge called "sacred sympath," we begin to blend with the forms of life and know, in inner experience, that on a deeper level we are truly one with all the forms of nature.

It is the over-masculinated faculties of intellect, seeing and analyzing the separate parts, that drive man into exploiting the animals and indulging in cruelty for his own advantage. Thus, he brutalizes himself and blunts his sensitivity. Compassion represents the more feminine side of our nature. ("Male and female created He them.") Compassion, (*Mit-leid*, "suffering with") awakens in the heart when the imaginative vision has "seen" the oneness of life.

Thus surely in the new society which is now emerging in the midst of our greedy egoistic materialist culture, a new sympathy for the sacredness of all life will be central. A great cleansing of the planet is now taking place. That which is evil and based merely on getting more for self is being dissolved by energies of harmony, seeping and flooding into human consciousness. There is a long way to go, but, if we take the notion, we can see how many new impulses for cooperation and compassion and caring are appearing in the New Age groupings and enterprises. The new society now emerging (dare we call it the New Jerusalem?) will be composed of people whose soul-quality is such that they will literally be unable to hurt life. They will no longer desire to hunt or shoot for fun; they will be incapable of the horrible processes of vivisection and will find alternative methods; they will revolt against factory farming and see it for the barbarism it really is.

Since creative living involves continuous and progressive cleansing and purification of soul and body as man spiritualizes his nature, it must follow that to eat animal flesh must bind him down to the animal vibration and impede his progress. Thus, to more and more people the eating of meat will become increasingly undesirable and even repulsive. The change all begins in our own thinking and in the development of an intuitive imagination which can grasp the oneness of all life and the divinity within all created things. Let us work to form a society of human beings who will accept their true status as attributes of God, taking the responsibility that comes with rational intelligence, and therefore accepting anew the God-given task of being stewards to the life on the planet. Of course we must fight our campaign to modify and change the evils that have arisen through human greed and ignorance. But the first essential is the inner change in understanding which will bring with it something of the poet's sensitivity of knowing that we are truly one with the beings and processes of nature. Then we shall know that we hurt ourselves when we hurt the animals. We begin individually and collectively to redeem the huge karmic debt with which our souls are loaded through our maltreatment and exploitation of the animal kingdom. Let us never forget that *cruelty is indivisible.* In the Oneness vision, we all share the responsibility and must start from within ourselves and our own environment to bring about the great redemption.

And be sure that there is a great spiritual brotherhood on the Higher Planes which will support our every effort.

12 | Alternative Lifestyle and the Holistic World View

Lᴇᴛ ᴜs ᴄᴏɴsɪᴅᴇʀ the different aspects of the movement towards an alternative lifestyle and see their significance in the light of the holistic world picture. This involves, as we have seen, a stretching of the imagination to grasp the concept of the oneness of all life, the living and organic nature of the Earth, the essentially spiritual nature of man and the universe and the belief that in these immediate years, an impulse for the harmonizing of all life is actually being released into human consciousness from higher realms of intelligence. This, if true, would prove to be the greatest source of hope for the redemption of mankind, but it is a factor wholly ignored in all ecological or economic discussion, since the materialistic intellectual outlook cannot admit to a great spiritual continuum of Being working "holistically" into our lives at every point. That word "holistic" is very significant, combining wholeness, holiness and healing. There can be no aspect of our lives not touched and influenced by the oneness of life. Axiomatically, its working must be everywhere, since we are all part of it. Therefore it can be helpful to learn to look at all problems in the light of this world view. Let us try to do so with regard to the "alternative lifestyle."

Quest for Meaning in Life

Many people in responsible positions are giving up their jobs in order to move away and do something they feel inherently worthwhile, often at the sacrifice of good salaries. Here is an urge to pause and find out what the meaning of life really is. Just "getting on" doesn't satisfy. This could very well be a sign of the impulse working within human consciousness, building up a dissatisfaction and a strange urge to find a new lifestyle. This seems usually to show itself in simplifying the way of living. When we look at our Western culture, we must admit to the reckless waste of resources, food, money, emotion and energy. Just think of the center of London or New York, Paris or Las Vegas, and see that we are burning up so much of Earth's resources every night in the extravagant pursuit of pleasure and desire. In imagination, look down upon Earth from space and see these flaming points in the rich North and West and the darkness of the southern continents in their poverty. Consider the advertising industry, mostly concerned with whipping up desire and creating an artificial sense of need so that we may spend more money to get more things — for someone's profit. Ours is an age when self-consciousness and egoism has developed to an acute degree. The tacit assumption is often that the only motive for work is the bigger wage package. Ours is a society largely geared to getting for self (or group), even at the price of doing the other fellow wrong. But many know there can be a quite other motive and that the salary is the necessary meeting of the need so that we may go on being creative— not a selling of our labor as a commodity.

The redemption of Earth calls for a turnabout in consciousness to rediscover this different motive for work in service of the Whole.

We may mention here the movement called Life-style *Commitment* now spreading in many countries. It recognizes that to save the world populations from starvation, it is necessary for the rich North and West to give to the poor South. But this is impossible so long as our economy is solely geared to profit. We don't know how to give the stuff away, so the wheat surplus is left to rot. The essential beginning must be through a change of attitude in the individual. It involves a commitment to a simplifying of lifestyle so as to cut out extravagant and wasteful use of resources and food in our own lives. Since there is still a lot of money about, this cutting down of meaningless expenditure releases funds for things which are really significant. The commitment includes the concept of tithing, i.e., deliberately setting aside a certain percentage of one's available income for others in real need. In some sense, this is a form of training of our own subconscious lower self. The movement has nothing dogmatic about it, but is a real sign of the workings of a new consciousness. It was launched in this country by the Dean of Bristol Cathedral, the Very Rev. Horace Dammers.

So important is it that Western man learns to share the produce of the earth that we are told to expect the embodiment of certain of the Masters, very exalted Beings who will be appearing in our midst to teach and help us to change lifestyle. We may recognize them by their vision and their universal love. Some would believe their appearance to be a prelude to the Second Coming.

Conservation

The broad movement for conservation may include Nature Conservancy, the Council for Preservation of Rural England, the Soil Association, Friends of the Earth and Men of the Trees. It is not in the least necessary for those working in these organizations to acknowledge the spiritual view of man and the universe here presented. They are working with the divine law of harmony of all life, whether they admit it or not. The holistic world view must see the Earth as a living organism, indeed a creature with its own breathing and bloodstream, glands and sensitivity, and an intelligence of which the human layer—the noosphere—is an essential part. We are not an accident in a nature wholly indifferent to mankind but are integrally part of the whole.

The oneness vision must recognize the sacredness of life and the divinity within all living things. As Blake said: "Every rock is deluged with Deity." For those who can see this, conservation takes on an almost priestly task in awakening people to responsible awareness of their duty as stewards of the planet. We are approaching the understanding that Mother Earth is a living being in a universe shot through and through with living thought and spirit. This conception heightens the meaning of every aspect of the conservation movement.

In our time, through spiritual research, we recover the knowledge of the etheric forces working within all nature, and the "eye of the mind," when thought is intensified to intuitive imagination, can begin to "see" the beings within natural form. Thus, we are recovering knowledge of the reality of the nature spirits and the elemental world, known to earlier cultures. Tomkins in his remarkable book *The Secret Life of Plants* describes research which reveals the astounding sensitivity of the plants. *The Findhorn Garden* is a book describing how a community in the north of Scotland first demonstrated the possibility of working in close cooperation with the nature spirits and devas by growing a wonderful garden of superb flowers and vegetables on arid windswept sand dunes. The implications are enormous. Man truly working with the elemental world could redeem the deserts. Man ignoring the nature spirits may turn the earth into a desert. And, of course, he must ignore them until he awakens to a vision beyond the limitations of his normal seeing. Hence, the importance of first grasping the spiritual world view of the oneness of life. Steiner's Biodynamic agriculture and horticulture is the most highly developed aspect of organic husbandry, and he was fully aware of the elemental world. He left a scientific approach which others can follow. Findhorn demonstrates the results of direct cooperation through consciously loving the plants and working under intuitive guidance from the devas. That garden is so important because it cannot be argued away. No other explanation is adequate to account for it on such an infertile site.

The science of Ecology is, of course, concerned with the interrelated working of life. But there is a long way to go before intellectual analysis can fully comprehend the incredible complexity of the pattern of life and nature.

Here we may see the importance of cooperation between the scientist and the adept or mystic, for the latter is one who can so lift consciousness that it attunes with the whole. Steiner demonstrated in his life and teaching that it was possible to intensify thinking so as to develop "sense-free thinking," which in imaginative cognition could unite with the world process and directly experience the Being within the form. This opened the door to a spiritual research as precise and accurate as the usual scientific investigation confined to demonstrable observation. Spiritual knowledge of the oneness of life will have ever increasingly to work with intellectual science to unravel the mysteries.

The whole movement for *Organic Husbandry* as represented by the Soil Association can be seen as an expression of this great impulse for man to work with the wholeness of Nature's working. It shows itself in a change of attitude from the "conquering of nature" to a cooperation with her in a new and nonviolent way. To quote Schumacher in *Small is Beautiful:*

> *The continuation of scientific advance in the direction of ever increasing violence, culminating in nuclear fission and moving on to nuclear fusion, is a prospect of terror threatening the abolition of man. Yet it is not written in the stars that this must be the direction. There is also a life-giving and life-enhancing possibility, the conscious exploration and cultivation of all relatively non-violent, harmonious, organic methods of cooperating with that enormous, wonderful incomprehensible system of God-given nature, of which we are a part and which we certainly have not made ourselves.*

Food Reform

Consider now the meaning of the movement for food reform. Almost all who are seeking a new life-pattern realize that they must change diet and eat "whole food." Ideally, we should be growing our own vegetables organically, but since only a limited number can achieve this, the development of Health Food shops and restaurants is a major aspect of the New Age movement. People mostly eat "too much, too soft, and too sweet." We may even see that we suffer from an "addiction" to cooked food. Ideally we should eat at least 80 per cent of our food raw, since cooking often kills the life in the food and upsets the incredibly delicate balance of vitamins, trace elements, amino acids and the like which is present in whole, uncooked food. In nutrition we are truly nourished by the life in the food. Steiner gave us a grace:

> *It is not the bread that nourisheth.*
> *What feeds us in the bread*
> *Is God's eternal word*
> *His spirit and His life.*

It is very significant to see how widespread in New Age groups is the ritual of grace and attunement before meals.

The aim should be consciously to eat things as near as possible to life and sunlight. The etheric energy is wholly lost in denatured, tinned, processed and overcooked food. Of course we are compelled to compromise. What matters is intelligent understanding. So much of the ill health of today is directly due to our putting toxic substances into our blood. The cleansing of the bloodstream through pure and whole food is the goal. Therefore, so many are becoming vegetarian and refusing to eat dead flesh. Therefore, so many are rejecting white bread for the wholemeal loaf. Therefore at last people begin to see the appalling dangers in eating quantities of refined white sugar. This is a wholly dead product. The average yearly intake in this country is 130 pounds—well over a hundredweight. Since many eat virtually no sugar at all, preferring honey, it must often be much higher. No wonder health is declining in so many directions. An important clue is to learn the art of conscious tasting. Chew the mouthful until you have pressed the last vestige of taste out of it. In a good wholemeal loaf, the pleasure of taste goes on increasing as the saliva gets mixed in with it, and you can virtually drink the resulting liquid. Thus you will naturally eat slower and are less likely to overeat. And you will increase enjoyment and will indeed notice the difference between live and dead food.

The change of diet towards whole and living food is integrally part of the wholeness vision of the New Age movement. Steiner even went so far as to say his spiritual teachings could not be understood unless we improved the quality of what we eat.

Holistic Healing and the Alternative Therapies

This is inherently part of the Alternative Lifestyle. Many are turning away from orthodox medicine to seek help in the approaches which are grounded in the holistic vision. These include Nature Cure and Food Reform, Hydrotherapy, Spiritual Healing, Radionics, Homoeopathy, Chiropractic and Osteopathy, Yoga and Massage, the Alexander Technique. These methods should rightly be seen as complementary to orthodox medicine. Already there is a movement for "Natural Health Centers" in many cities and towns, in which patients may take medical advice together with other alternative therapies. This may prove to be the beginnings of a true "Health Service," encouraging people to take full and creative responsibility for themselves and learn that positive health is a condition they can achieve through right living and right thought, without having recourse to drugs.

The Inner Game and The Great Sports

Now let us think about the remarkable developments in the last years in athletics and the great sports. The first book to appear was *Zen in the Art of Archery.* That was some fifteen years ago, but it clearly suggested that the attainment of skill was a far profounder affair than we had imagined. Then came Michael Murphy's *Golf in the Kingdom* and now a spate of books on what is being called the Inner Game, in skiing, tennis, swimming, athletics, climbing, gliding. A new vision emerges, and with it comes a continuous extending of the frontiers of performance until it seems there is no limit to what this marvelous instrument, the human body, can do and achieve and endure, not only in refinement of athletics and gymnastics, but in expeditions exploring the mountains, deserts and seas. Sport, at first sight, may seem little related to the spiritual world view. But apply the concept of wholeness. Man in essence is a free-ranging spiritual being entering embodiment in the dense gravity field of earth. This body is a quite miraculous piece of design by the Creative Source. The spiritual entity, the I, is learning ever more consciously to control it, to direct its energies and explore its potentialities. The body is much more than a machine. It is a sensitized point of Earth, a bridging point between two worlds—the gravity field of matter and the ethereal realms of eternal spirit. We begin to grasp what has been forgotten in the last rational centuries—that there is a primary polarity between gravity and anti-gravity or "levity." These two forces meet in perfect balance on the surface of the earth, working throughout living nature and are chiefly demonstrated in the human organism. The leg is given over wholly to gravity and the poised head on the vertical spine is lifted into levity and open to cosmic thinking. Arms are freed to use tools or express emotion. As the Essenes knew of old, man is at every point and at all times in touch with the great oceans of energy, Wisdom and Power. To the degree that we can attune, we can work creatively with these energies which are alive and angelic in their nature. By "angelic," we imply that these are not merely mechanical forces but are living and operative. The holistic vision sees that the universe is shot through and through with weaving fields of energy, which, being everywhere, are here and available to each of us, could we but learn how to tap these endless reservoirs.

So we see the deeper significance of the "Inner Game." It involves the recognition that thought and imagination is a creative force. Conscious direction of energy and the ability to act into new thought patterns of movement releases undreamt of possibility of ever-advancing achievement. Conscious direction of the use of the self can enhance any athletic form.

Here we must acknowledge the place of the *Alexander Technique and Principle.* F. M. Alexander, before the War, was teaching his discovery of the "primary control" as a means of rectifying habits of wrong use which by familiarity had come to "feel" right. It is a fundamental teaching of conscious constructive control of the use of the body as a working whole. It will in time be recognized that this is basic to healthy living, and that, when applied to any sport, it will result in a notable enhancing of achievement.

The Body as Temple

The oneness view must see the body as truly the temple into which the spiritual can descend. The inner *cela* of the Greek temple was the chamber in which Apollo or Athene could touch down, without being contaminated by gravity. So we may see the body as the sacred temple for the spark of God to operate. As a spiritual entity we can, through the body, enjoy and explore the world. We are not our bodies but, rather, live through them and so can refine their sensitivity and extend achievement.

The great sports when looked at in this way are seen as a means of consciously coming into relation with the living elements—earth, air, fire and water. The ancient concept still holds good. Air and fire manifest the centrifugal field of levity; water and earth the field of gravity. Thus sailing, skin-diving and canoeing relate us to water. The face mask and aqualung open a world of wonder and beauty. Cave exploring brings us into the mystery of earth. The intense fascination of this searching out of the secrets of the earth and finding the shining temples of stalactite in the Stygian darkness can involve a heightening of consciousness. For we must grasp that the world of crystals and minerals is in fact related to the highest of the spiritual hierarchies. Witness the occult knowledge of many of the old miners. Mountaineering in all its degrees of severity holds for so many a sense of the mystery of high hills. Think into the Earth as a sentient creature. Feel the lure of the hills and the grandeur of the great heights and the endless challenge offered by rock and ice. To admit to the spirit of the hills is not, of course, necessary in following the sport. But those who can extend imaginative intuition will sense that certain hills hold power and are holy places. "I will lift up mine eyes unto the hills, from whence cometh my help."

In primeval days, Earth was much more alive and divinity active in creation. Rock was first living substance, deposited and hardened into the dead skeleton of the globe. In a deep sense, the mountains were sentient beings and to this day may hold a dormant power and low consciousness. Wordsworth knew this when he wrote:

> *And I have felt*
> *A presence that disturbs me with the joy*
> *Of elevated thoughts; a sense sublime*
> *Of something far more deeply interfused,*
> *Whose dwelling is the light of setting suns,*
> *And the round ocean and the living air,*
> *And the blue sky, and in the mind of man:*
> *A motion and a spirit, that impels*
> *All thinking things, all objects of all thought,*
> *And rolls through all things.*

In these great sports we are, physically and imaginatively, becoming one with the elements, and the experience can be enriched if we grasp our oneness with earth and air. Hang-gliding clearly brings us nearest to the experience of bird flight; apparently the flyer can "feel" to the very wing tip, as if they were truly extensions of his sensory and nervous mechanism. The great airmen and astronauts have frequently confessed to the sense of the presence of God, as when Edgar Michell, emerging from behind the moon and seeing Earth again, had the peak experience in which he knew with inner certainty that the universe was an affair of consciousness working to Divine Law. Life to him thereafter could never be the same. He had recovered the sense of meaning.

We see in our time the great development of the mountain schools like Plas-y-Brenin in Snowdonia and the adventure centers for escape from the cities into the high lands in order to come to terms with nature and our own capacity for endurance.

In our generation, the great sports are open to everyone with the drive and enterprise, for finance no longer limits them to the fortunate elite. But for the more deprived in the great cities, there is a movement afoot for the "Endeavour" schemes which show how groups can come together in every kind of setting and with the right initial lead, devise their own form of enterprise.

Survival Techniques

Obviously, work in this field could become supremely important if world conditions become grim. The group which recently lived a year in conditions of stone age man have certainly given a remarkable demonstration. The significance is fully realized if we see that the present tribulations may be the prelude to a rebirth of a New Age. The spiritual world view shows us that the essence of man, the I, is immortal and not subject to death. Therefore, however catastrophic the coming changes, life goes on for us all on one level or another. Souls released from the body will move on to a higher plane. After the cleansing of the planet, the rebuilding operation begins. So the centers learning the arts of survival may be serving a greater purpose than merely saving their own skins. After all, Noah was the master of that art and we owe him a debt of gratitude!

Meditation Groups

It is true that the use of imaginative visualization in meditation can become a genuine exploration of inner space. Meditation is the entry into the stilled center within our consciousness, the gateway through which we can expand into the worlds of higher awareness. It thus takes a profoundly important place in the emerging of the new lifestyle. Many different forms are being taught and practiced. Groups are springing up everywhere, but all have the same basic goal—to create a still center which can open up towards the inflooding of the light of a higher consciousness. As Browning expressed it: "There is an inmost center in us all where Truth abides in fullness." It is the greatest treasure we can possess. It is the pearl of great price, through which in time we shall learn to attune to our Higher Self, the I AM. When the lower personality with its ego-drives is subordinated to the Higher Self, then the possibility opens for a man or woman to become creative as never before, for we shall in full consciousness be tapping the reservoirs of living ideas and allowing ourselves to become active channels for the creative source. This is the ultimate purpose of man's sojourn upon earth, the great training ground for souls. Such surrender to the Higher Self in service of the whole will prove to be an enhancement of all creative talents, for we are working with Him "whose service is perfect freedom."

The Adventure Sports

In recent years, there has been a striking increase in the range of adventurous exploration of the mountains, the seas and, indeed, the skies. Remarkable feats have been achieved by small expeditions in the Himalayas and The Andes. Everest has been climbed solo and without oxygen. Canoeists have rounded Cape Horn and now are tackling the wild waters of some of the highest and toughest rivers in the Himalayas. The circumnavigation of the globe by the sailing ship "Eye of the Wind," so rightly called "Operation Drake," has been triumphantly completed. The Adventure Sports indeed demonstrate a wealth of enterprise and achievement.

Surely we may see this as an aspect of the awakening of the

Planet. The separate particle, that tiny speck of human consciousness, is discovering that it is indeed an integral part of the Whole and that awareness and achievement can be extended indefinitely. When we explore, whether in physical adventure or inwardly in mental widening through meditation, it is as if the consciousness of the Whole is quickened. Our body is the focal point for consciousness which can dilate itself and move out into ethereal realms. Charles J. Earle expresses this thought in a sonnet:

> *The body is not bounded by its skin,*
> *Its effluence, like a gentle cloud of scent,*
> *Is wide into the air diffused, and blent*
> *With elements unseen, its way doth win*
> *To ether frontiers, where take origin*
> *Far subtler systems, nobler regions, meant*
> *To be the area and the instrument*
> *of operations ever to begin anew*
> *And never end. Thus every man*
> *Wears as his robe the garment of the sky,*
> *So close his union with the cosmic plan,*
> *So perfectly he pierces low and high,*
> *Reaching as far in space as creature can*
> *And co-extending with immensity.*

All mountaineers must at times have felt very near to The Being of Earth. We are justified, if we so wish, in feeling the validity of a "mystique" of mountaineering. Climbing, after all, can be experienced as an allegory upon the whole of life. This is a subtler aspect of its delight.

The Crafts

A kindred symptom is the revival of interest in the crafts. Many of those who leave the great cities and the "rat-race" and seek to live the "good life" are practicing crafts. This, of course, is a satisfying occupation, but it can also be seen in the greater context of holism. Just as the great sports bring us into intimate relation with the elements, so the crafts relate us to matter and substance. Think for instance of pottery. We take the most basic and inert of things—clay. We shape it quickly with the hand into beauty of form. We add mineral in the glaze and put the product into its sarcophagus of the kiln and apply fire. Then the wonderful metamorphosis takes place and we open the tomb and reveal the hidden treasure shining with beauty and color. Then we use it for food and drink and the ritual of breaking bread together. Indeed, the whole thing, if you wish, is a kind of ritual. In like manner, we can comtemplate what it really means to make furniture out of wood or raise a metal bowl or work in silver and gold or forge iron. These metals in the earth are indeed functions of the planetary forces—iron of Mars, silver of the Moon, gold of the Sun. No wonder man has a lust for gold, distorted by greed, but in reality a quest for the source of life. We are working with aspects of the living earth and shaping them in beauty.

To quote D. H. Lawrence:

> *Things men have made with wakened hands, and put soft life into are awake through years with transferred touch, and go on glowing for long years. And for this reason, some old things are lovely, warm still with the life of forgotten men who made them.*

Let it not be thought that talk about simplifying life-style and practicing crafts implies that the New Age movement is merely a return to the simple life. Obviously, this is impossible for all in our culture. The new communities can also use electronic devices to reduce the burden of labor. Indeed, we must face up to the implication of the coming revolution in microprocessing and mini-computers. This will cause major changes in our society and could greatly increase the amount of leisure. Then the real educational problem will be of paramount importance—how do we increase the sense of meaning in life so as to awaken a drive and enthusiasm in new creativity. The "silicon chips" may prove to be an aspect of the whole transforming process, driving us into a new lifestyle, negative or positive in its effects according to our use of intelligence and vision.

Here also let us admit the great opportunity brought about by the extension of expectation of life. The senior citizen now has perhaps a dozen free years to use after retirement or the launching of a family. Such a condition has never previously been known in history. Some are bored and lost in their leisure, but it may be seen as a profoundly significant chance to deepen wisdom in preparation for the great release of so-called "death," which too many people enter with all too little understanding. Adult education in its real sense never comes to an end. "Is not the whole of Eternity mine?" (Lessing).

New Experiments in Community Living

The new thinking draws people to try and work out the new lifestyle in group endeavor. Some are small—and indeed it is right to begin small and develop organically. The most important example of the successful community in this country is Findhorn. This also started from the smallest unit, but from the first was a demonstration of working not for self but for the Whole, to the glory of God and under divine guidance. At present there are some 200 permanent members, and very many come on training courses. It is also a demonstration of "the Law of Manifestation," so vital in our days of economic difficulty. It shows that when a group is genuinely dedicated to the service of God, the real needs will be met—not our wants and desires but His needs through us in the service which only we can fulfill. These needs are fulfilled to perfection, since in God is abundance. It is a precarious way of living, but it may be a clue for many in the coming period of change when the economic structure of our society seems to be breaking down. For the implication of the holistic world picture is that "Operation Redemption" has now been launched. This implies that the energies that vitalized the old social structure based on getting for self are being withdrawn, and in their place are being released living energies that are inherently powered for the harmonizing of all life with the workings of divine law. If we can take this concept, may it not throw light on the present symptoms of breakdown, which could fill us with dismay unless we can accept that dying is always a necessary prelude to renewal, making way for the inflooding of transforming forces which could bring to birth a new society.

Then indeed we see the meaning of these community experiments in a new lifestyle. These are like the first snowdrops appearing or the first shoots of self-sown oak or beech trees. They are tender things which can be crushed by a heavy boot, but we know that the force behind them is absolutely irresistible. Spring must come and nothing can stop it. After the death of winter comes the renewal. The analogy is good. Imagine that each little snowdrop or tiny oak tree is conscious and comes to feel itself very much alone and isolated. Then it becomes aware that all over the wood are others of the same sort. It is part of a wide movement which can be coordinated. So it is with all the endeavors we have been considering. They are symptoms of the quickening of the spirit in our time. Behind them is a tremendous power, the coming of the Light.

The terrible darkness of our present world may indeed be the last stand of the great negator against the inflooding of the Aquarian Age. This hope brings a joy in a time of dismay. It may be serving a really important function if these regional groups link with each other and come together every now and then to look at what they are doing in the light of the greater picture. For the spirit has no meaning if it is working *in vacuo* and detached from life. It is not airy nothing. It is the divine force of life which plays down into every aspect of our earth existence and is capable of transforming our society and our ways of working. But always human initiative is essential. This is the great paradox. We have not been saying that we have to wait on God to take over. His Will is that we learn to use our own will creatively in His service.

13 | Operation Redemption

THIS FINAL CHAPTER begins with the last reading in Leonora Nichols' *Within the Fountain:*

> *One message runs through all these communications like a shining thread of gold and each brings a variation on the one theme. And what is that theme but the Eternal Truth that I AM here, within thee, I, the Living God. Thou who are man, man of my creating, art the beloved Son, even as Christ revealed.*
>
> *The denial of this truth is the darkness spreading over the face of the earth.*
>
> *I speak now to those who have ears to hear, who offer their hearts in love and service and thereby have the capacity to listen to My Voice speaking in the stillness of their deeper Self-hood. And I say the hour has come for the fulfilling of the Law, both in the destruction of those forces that deny and defame it, and in the liberation of those energies that affirm and fulfill it.*
>
> *Even so must it be, for there is sowing and reaping and this is the working out of the Law that changeth not.*
>
> *O thou who art listening, who art the sons and daughters of God, be not dismayed, for so will a New Peace spread out over the world, and upon this Peace rests the Tabernacle of the New Jerusalem or the New Day on earth. Amen.*

Such is the scale of our time. Either these ideas are so much nonsense and delusion, or they are of supreme significance. Each of us will decide.

If you have reached this far, you will probably be able to take this final chapter. We have looked at the holistic world view and applied it to a number of aspects of our living. Now let us do the same for that great issue of the next two decades—the looming threat of world catastrophe. This will indeed involve stretching the imagination into realms that may at first sight appear fantasy. But remember what has been so often stressed—that there is no demand for belief, but rather the readiness to entertain new ideas and let them work in us while reserving judgment. For these ideas clearly bring a vision of hope in a turbulent age. So please read on and follow the holistic viewpoint to what may be its logical conclusion.

It is all too clear that the next decades are pregnant with possibilities of change. What sort of world are we offering our children? We should look with the vision of wholeness at the prospects ahead of us in the immediate coming years. We all know of the doom-talk. This is not the place to go deeper into it. The potential disasters, political, economic, climatic and in the structure of the Earth, are well written up in such books as Ronald Higgins' *The Seventh Enemy* and Jeffrey Goodman's *The Earthquake Generation*. Powerful reading indeed! We are more concerned with what is foretold by many great seers and spiritual researchers, that the end of the twentieth century will mark a turning point in human evolution, opening many people to a new dimension of spiritual vision and therefore bringing to birth a new age. This is obviously a prospect full of great hope, yet when we look at our present society, it seems a far cry! Therefore, it implies that there must be major changes to transform and sweep away the negative forces which so strongly maintain their grip on the present life-pattern.

There have been many communications received by sensitives from the realms of higher consciousness, warning mankind of the prospects of disaster if he continues unchecked on his reckless, downhill path of materialism, rivalry and war. But we must see the complementary role of prophet and priest; the former has the task of awakening us to the inevitable end of our egoistic exploitation of earth resources. Prophecies are couched in terms as if they are certainly going to happen, since their function is to shake us and awaken us. But they need not happen and can be avoided. The priestly task is to show the great hope that comes if we can achieve a turnabout in consciousness and cooperate with the heavenly forces to bring about the New Age.

This, then, seems to be the situation:

Mankind has polluted the planet Earth as a direct result of greedy egoism in a society primarily based on individual and group rivalry and drive for power. It is probable that the world problems of pollution have already gone so far that they are insoluble if we continue to face them as if the Earth were a dead thing in a mechanistic universe. Our understanding is too limited. There is little hope of avoiding calamitous change until we really begin to *think* wholeness and then to *act* wholeness.

This leads us on to an apocalyptic world picture, and here lies the great hope. The world is so mad and bad and so fraught with danger that it is surely justifiable to grasp with our thinking the sublime possibility of creative change and cleansing of the planet. Let us welcome change as a force essential to the bringing in of the new. So long as our primary concern is to keep things as they are and hold on to what we have at all costs, then we shall bring disaster upon ourselves. The changes envisaged by the Communist "take-over bid" are still materialistic. They take no cognizance of the living divine whole. The apocalyptic picture does just that. Let us bravely look at it as a positive alternative. It implies that we are overlooking a major factor and ignoring our chief allies, without whose help our planetary problems are probably insoluble. The significance of this factor, implicit in the vision of the oneness of all life, is of course ignored by our governments and by economists, technologists and even ecologists. It is still largely felt to be irrelevant to take the spiritual worlds into consideration. The truth is that human self-sufficiency alone is inadequate but that the real help is there if we can but see it and invoke it.

The wholeness world view implies, as we have already said, that planet Earth is a living creature, an organism within the greater organism of the solar system. We compared it with one of the endocrine glands, those tiny centers which control the health of the whole body. So it is with the planets circling the Sun. One of them has gone dark. Through human greed and ignorance, grave damage has been done and Earth is dying.

How long may we expect the greater organism to tolerate this irritant, this pain within its body? We have seen that the cosmos is an affair of consciousness, shot through and through with divine thought and being. These oceans of life and wisdom are fields of energy called angelic in the sense used by the Essenes. The whole could clearly pour in its power to cleanse and heal the part, by water or fire or molecular change. Man, great in his play with his toys, is obviously puny when faced with the mighty power of cosmic energy and the thought of Intelligences far ahead of our own.

Here I recommend Kit Peddler's challenging book *The Quest for Gaia*. Gaia, in Greek mythology, is the Earth Goddess. It is helpful to think of her again to explain what we really mean by speaking of the "living Earth." It appears that Gaia has a power of stabilizing and balancing the seething mass of life in constant change and motion. This works as an integrated whole, all its myriad species and operations perpetually brought into dynamic relationship by what Peddler characterizes as the intelligence of the Earth Goddess. This is able to sense where some attack threatens the harmonious balanced interchange of energies and can parry and neutralize the threat. Her life rhythms may be slow, but sooner or later she will stabilize herself. Industrial man, in this brief period of a couple of centuries out of millions of years of evolution, threatens now to unstabilize the whole. This is because he no longer works directly with the "solar drive chain," but relies on stored solar energy of the fossil fuels. The result of this is an enormous increase of entropy, i.e., the percentage of heat waste involved in any technological process. The entropic leak from preindustrial society was relatively small and could be stabilized by Earth relying on Sun energy direct. Mankind's lifestyle was closely related to the Earth Rhythms. Now industrial man, in what Peddler calls his "technological toymaking," has wholly forgotten Gaia and is recklessly using up world resources without any thinking of wholeness. There comes the point when Gaia can no longer tolerate parasite man, her faulty steward. Atmospheric and seismographic changes may be seen as a form of protest by the Earth. Ultimately, her strength is such that nothing could withstand it. Peddler illustrates this by the way in which bacteria can breed immunity to poison sprays and lethal drugs and, as is now being shown, are able even to transfer this knowledge of resistance through cellular contact to other species. The stronger the attack, the more powerful the resistance it calls forth. If we as a race are to survive, there is no choice but to turn about and begin living again with Gaia, consciously planning our lifestyle to avoid the entropy which is bleeding energy out of the body of the earth. Hence the profound significance of all the current movements for an alternative lifestyle as described in an earlier chapter. These are not cranky fads or fancies but the beginnings of a movement which must spread throughout human society if as a race we are to survive.

The planet must be cleansed. We as men could be the chief instruments. It would be a glorious triumph if now there could come a turnabout in consciousness so that with our own intelligence we could wake up to the unity of all life and reform our lifestyle to conform with it.

But anyway, planet Earth is to be cleansed. This now seems to be the primal issue, if we are to believe the communications. Time is running out, and the forces of the divine intelligence must go into action.

We must remember always that mankind has been given free

will. The developing of the Tenth Hierarchy has been one of the divine projects—human beings worthy in time to stand as friends of God and co-creators with him. This means that human potential is unlimited, if once the transforming step has been taken in consciousness to unite human intelligence with the ocean of creative wisdom. This could bring about a veritable new Renaissance, greater than that of the fifteenth century, since it would involve mankind uniting in enhanced thinking with the realm of creative Ideas. That this great step forward should be achieved, a sweeping away of the clutter and debris of materialistic egoism has first to take place. The celestial forces could clear pollution, if they so chose, by instant molecular change, but it must be accepted that the powers of the Archangel Michael, respecting human freedom, may not take over without our cooperation and invocation. Once we call on them, as individuals, groups, or even nations, then they can immediately respond and the human soul would be filled with strength and joy, knowing itself to be an instrument for the working of divine redemption. The invasion has been sounded. The infiltration has already begun. Those who "know" may be likened to a fifth column in an enemy-occupied country. Too few have as yet become aware of the remarkable things now developing behind the outward facade of current events. We can foresee a build-up of desperate tension as the forces of negation struggle to maintain their stranglehold on the human spirit. Then may come a collapse and disintegration both of social structure and of outdated thought forms, but into the vacuum will then flood a counter-force of the Light, washing away the negative, as when a dam bursts and the torrent takes over, and lifting and uniting all souls who have won through to the new understanding.

How long the period of change is to be is obviously impossible to foretell, and even those on "the other side" admit that they cannot be certain. There will be a turning point, and this is approaching, but the process of entering the New Age may, of course, be extended over a number of years. The most important news is that the battle for the Light has already been won on the higher planes. The ultimate victory is certain, according to many sources of communication. The degree of distress during the working-out on the earth plane depends entirely on the degree of human understanding and cooperation with the inflooding forces of the Light. This, of course, is implied in the allegory of the Apocalypse:

> *And there was war in heaven: Michael and his angels fought against the dragon and the dragon fought and his angels and prevailed not. And the great dragon was cast out into the earth . . . having great wrath, because he knoweth that he hath but a short time.*

Indeed, to make sense of the present world situation we should learn to see it apocalyptically. We have spoken of this already in the chapter on the Second Coming. Here indeed lies the supreme hope that follows tribulation.

We know that death for the true entity of man is an illusion, for the "I" is immortal and imperishable. Thus death is the great educator, through the breaking down of the perishable sheath which temporarily houses the deathless spirit. Our dread of catastrophe is of course colored by the fear of death. But once we grasp the spiritual world conception, we know that it makes little difference whether we are on this plane or the next. Let us admit that a great tidal wave would be the quickest way to the New Jerusalem! For the immortal soul, it will be much more comfortable to be on the higher plane and released from the restrictions of earth life! The important thing now is that we each try to think through to the full scale of the possible events approaching us. How grave these events are to be depends entirely on the degree of human cooperation with the forces which are bringing about the changes. These in their power and action may appear quite ruthless, for Earth is to be cleansed. It is vital that we should reach up to grasp the spiritual world picture, with a deep certainty that God knows what he is doing in allowing mankind to indulge in evil and violence. He waits for our awakening and his timing is perfect.

The mystical truth is expressed in John 15:16, John 4:19, and Phil. 4:13: ''You did not choose me—but I chose you.'' ''We love God because He first loves us.'' For ultimate Reality is dynamic. It moves towards us as we move towards it. As Paul expressed it: ''I can do all things through Christ which strengtheneth me.'' Yet human initiative always remains the essential factor.

> *From the center that we call the Race of Men*
> *Let the Plan of Love and Light work out.*

We can invoke the Light and offer ourselves as creative channels for its working. Then we may be certain we are under the protection and guidance of our Higher Self, our angels and our friends out of the body. Then we can move into times of change with an inner attunement. We can dare to throw ourselves bravely on the intuitive guidance of the moment, knowing that in crisis or bewilderment, our invisible friends are very near with their support. If they want us still on this earth plane, we shall be moved out of danger. There is no need to scramble to save our skin if we believe we are being aided. Equally, when we are needed on the next plane, we shall be led into circumstances which free us from the body and release us for wider action. It appears (if we can take it) that the timing of death is always perfect.

We must remember that death is not the end. The soul freed from its body, by whatever event, will rally to those beings to whom it is attuned. Therefore, the souls attuned to the powers of light and love will be drawn by attraction on to a plane of being with kindred souls. Those who are still bound to the old law of getting for self will be shepherded on to some other planetary level, to be given their opportunity again at a later round, while some who have remained on a very low evolutionary level may be returned to what is called the soul pool.

Meaning is given to a time of potentially catastrophic change if we can conceive it on this scale. In our strange time almost anything is possible. Surely our world has something of the fantastic character of science fiction. We continue our daily lives and pursuits knowing that nuclear bombs are being proliferated which could destroy our civilization many times over, and in addition, human ingenuity is devising forms of germ and nerve gas warfare too horrible for most of us to imagine and all because of the fear and greed inherent in the unreformed egoism of mankind. The situation is indeed so grave that we are surely justified in entertaining a counter view—that there are possibilities just as fantastic which might involve the redemption and transformation of man.

It has been said by a wise teacher that "There are only two kinds of people today—those who know and those who don't want to know." Does this seem too severe on the many who have not met or concerned themselves with these "New Age" ideas? It may, however, be that on some deeper level every soul has made its inner choice. Perhaps in these last years, the angelic world has been devising ways of penetrating the auras of everyone, so that when the sword of Michael strikes, each will know on which side he or she stands—for the old way or for the New Jerusalem coming to birth. After all, to have read some science fiction (perhaps inspired by higher worlds), to have read Tolkein's saga *The Lord of the Rings*, or to have seen the film *Close Encounters of the Third Kind*, is enough to plant in the soul the sense of the possibility of levels of intelligence far beyond our own.

Once you admit this, the doorway is open to a new and wider understanding. If and when the changes begin, each soul will experience either misgiving and fear or a welling up of strange joy which will make the heart leap in the wild hope that redemption is near. May this not prove to be the ultimate in wonder and marvel? May it be that the raising of consciousness could come "in the twinkling of an eye," as implied in Scripture? Are we not justified in gambling everything on the supreme hope of such a change bringing redemption, since the alternative prospects are so sinister? Even if we are wrong, we certainly get a run for our money and the fun of anticipation before we are snuffed out! And if we are right, then how desperate we should feel if, on our passing into the life beyond, our friends and angelic guides were able to say: "Look at what we showed you, all the hints and signs we gave you, the wonderful and true ideas you imagined and *yet* you didn't have the courage to ally yourselves with us." Let us avoid *that* remorse, which would be devastating to the soul. And never forget that we were shown our destiny before we descended into earth embodiment.

Thus we may assume that those who have associated themselves with the spiritual movement for the New Age must assuredly have had a preview of the stupendous events of the closing decades of the century and have consciously undertaken the task of living through this great period. This thought is of especial importance for the young. Of course we forget what we knew before descending into birth, but many respond to the New Age vision because deep in their soul they know its truth. What a generation in which to be alive!

"Without vision the people perish." True enough, but: "Look up, for your redemption draweth nigh."

The Second Coming seems to be central to the picture. As we have said in another chapter, it is dangerous to speculate too precisely on what form this will take, but *expectancy* is the note of the hour. As Teilhard wrote in *Le Milieu Divin:*

> *Expectation—anxious, collective and operative expectation of an*
> *end of the world, that is to say of an issue for the world—that is the*

supreme function and most distinctive characteristic of our religion.

What then does the "Christ impulse" mean? The Christ is the Avatar of Love, the Savior who comes to all men in response to the call of desperate human need. Christ brought a new impulse of Love. Before his day, love and hate were bound up with blood relationship. Tribe or clan loved and hated through the blood. The Christ love could transcend all barriers and create a new bond between individual egos. This is why Hitler's doctrine of racialism was so retrograde, an attempt to reverse the progressive trend into the love-bond between individual souls of any race. The impulse carries mankind forward towards becoming one human family, blending races and cultures so that a true unity in diversity may be achieved. The Sun Spirit, the Logos, becomes flesh, descends into the human heart. The Risen Christ (by whatever name we call Him) works from soul to soul from within. He is concerned not only with one religion but with all mankind. But though individuals become Christian and confess to Christ, the national and racial group remains, as it were, unbaptized. Is Britain *as a nation* really Christian? The Folk-Soul remains uncommitted. As yet, a whole people dedicated to Christ does not exist except as a Utopian dream.

Now it is an important aspect of the Mystery of the Grail that it brings an impulse which will lead to The Christ working into the Folk-Souls of the nations. This would be an event of profound significance in evolution. The Folk-Souls are like great archangelic Beings. We have to imagine a family of Folk-Souls working on a high plane in harmony to fulfill the destiny of the human race. We have the qualities which make us English or French or Dutch through each of us being attributes of the Folk-Soul. Thus, the mixed races merge and grow into one to make Americans or Britons. The next great evolutionary step, be it repeated, could be for the Christ to enter and take over the Folk-Souls.

Here use your science-fiction imagination. Conceive that at midnight tonight, the supreme event took place. We should awake with a sense of a deep inner change. Those who were concerned with violence, crime or lust for power would be thrown into fear and confusion. Those whose auras were open to the impregnation would be filled with supreme joy. Love would flow out from each to all beings. This could happen. Chesterton's fine hymn expresses it.

> *Tie in a living tether*
> > *The prince and priest and thrall*
> *Bind all our lives together*
> > *Smite us and save us all.*
> *In ire and exultation*
> > *Aflame with faith and free*
> *Lift up a living nation*
> > *A single sword to thee.*

Then we should know that in our desperate need, there is no ultimate protection but in Christ. Suppose that, as a national impulse of the entire Folk-Soul, we acted on this thought—not another futile treaty on arms limitation, but a revulsion of feeling against more slaughter, a mass decision that we should no longer be party to the monstrous folly of war and are not prepared to take on ourselves the karma of mass murder.

Idealism, of course, but valid perhaps against the backcloth of nuclear war which neither side could "win."

May I quote from a book *Secret of the Andes* by Brother Philip. This describes a supposed monastic center deep in the Andes and includes a number of archangelic pronouncements telepathically received. Here is one purporting to come from the Archangel Gabriel, describing what will happen if man should go into major war. This statement must, to the rational mind, seem obviously absurd or at least wildly improbable. I quote it, not because I be-

lieve (or disbelieve) it, but because it presents a kind of challenge
to us to keep an open mind and reserve judgment in the face of
the improbable. It really looks as if much that is happening now is
planned from higher levels of intelligence to shock us out of our
absolute reliance on logical intellect and compel us to break
through in thought into a different dimension, another reality.
With this in mind, read "Gabriel's" warning when Armageddon
comes:

> *The armies shall be stopped by a great natural cataclysm. The
> weapons shall melt in their hands. They will find finally that the
> Earth has reached the place where the vibrations will no longer
> tolerate an act of wanton murder on the part of its inhabitants. For
> centuries man has spilled blood upon the Earth. Now the vibration
> refuses to kill. In the great war when man raises his weapons
> against his fellow men, they will not function in the new vibration.
> Anything that will cause destruction will melt. If a man utters a
> destructive word, he will disintegrate. Everything negative will
> vanish . . . Your country is not Christian. It is not following the
> Master Jesus. If it was, it would lay down arms and destroy all its
> atomic weapons. It would have no weapons of destruction or pro-
> tection. It would rely on Him alone to protect them. He is the only
> protection.*

Hold the logical mind in control and let the imagination play.
There is nothing inherently impossible in this extraordinary statement in a Universe woven through with divine power and creative thought. Perhaps there is already a precedent. Remember
that during the desperate days of the evacuation of the B.E.F.
from the Dunkirk beaches, a National Day of Prayer was called by
the Archbishop of Canterbury. It seemed indeed like a miracle
that within the seven days of the evacuation, 225,000 British offi-
cers and men and 103,000 of our French and Belgian allies were
brought safely away from apparently certain disaster. A member

of the Government publicly declared: "A miracle is happening. It is incredible beyond our wildest hopes. Our prayers have been answered." Then through the initiative of Wellesley Tudor-Pole and with the support of Churchill and the King, the "Big Ben Silent Minute" was instigated by BBC Radio during the striking of Big Ben at 9 p.m. Thus millions around the world united in prayer for protection of this island in the time of desperate need. After the war, a high-ranking German officer was asked in interrogation why the invasion of Britain failed. He replied: "You had a secret weapon which we could never understand, but which we knew was somehow associated with the striking of Big Ben."

There are also stories from the Battle of Britain that captured German pilots were asked why they turned back when they had 200 bombers against a dozen Spitfires. The answer, in some astonishment, was that they saw not a dozen but scores of fighters coming at them out of the sun. And, further, consider the implications of the secret science of Huna, discussed briefly in another chapter. The life force, Mana, collected by the low self and offered as a gift to the Higher Self in support of a prayer, gives a power which, converted into "High Mana," is able to bring about instant molecular change. This was constantly demonstrated by the Kahunas in their healing, even to the restoring of crushed and broken bones to perfect condition. Max Freedom Long, author of the books on Huna, joined with his colleagues in the "Huna Research Association" to offer protection through Huna-type prayer to their young men then fighting in the Korean War. It seems that they came unscathed through heavy machine gun fire, when all around them were falling. Long seriously believed that they were building a sheath of High Mana around the young soldier so that when the bullet reached its mark, it would actually dematerialize and pass harmlessly through the body in this state, to reform behind his back and proceed on its way!

We are, indeed, in a world of white magic. Now take these two illustrations and combine them. Britain was surrounded in 1940 by a wall of prayer, and the young airmen of "The Few" were given strength to achieve the impossible. Suppose now that the Folk-Soul of Britain were taken over and fully impregnated with the Christ power, so that all its members were also filled with a universal compassion and love. If then, as a nation, this country refused to involve itself with killing and threw itself solely on the Divine protection of the Living Christ, the land would be surrounded and covered by a dome and shield of High Mana.

Like to a moat defensive to a house
Against the envy of less happier lands.
(Richard II)

Then (O science fiction!) the Russian rockets fired at our unresisting land, would, when they reached the protective barrier, simply disappear! The situation would be so dramatic, so totally contrary to rational and logical thinking, that the Divine Power could no longer be ignored and would have to be admitted. The agony of tension and despair would be converted into exultant joy. If *God is*, then nothing is impossible to Him. Then such a situation is by no means out of the realm of possibility. Even to conceive it is a good exercise in flexibility of mind and certainly gives us food for optimistic thinking.

The portents and prophecies of our time, if rightly read, are seen as warnings shot through with a hope so extraordinary that we must try to stretch our thinking to encompass it. It is wise to reserve judgment, to watch, to pray, to expect, to hope, to be innerly still and to listen. Something is surely happening—anything could happen. This is not in any sense put forward as a policy for a Government or party to follow. It is a Truth which might in certain circumstances fulfill itself—in wonder. We are free to imbue our minds with it—or reject it as utterly absurd. But let us face the reality—THERE IS NO DEFENCE AGAINST NUCLEAR ATTACK.

For heathen heart that puts her trust
In reeking tube and iron shard,
All-valiant dust that builds on dust
And guarding calls not Thee to guard.
For frantic boast and foolish word—
Thy mercy on Thy people, Lord!
(Kipling)

Awake awake, the world is young
For all its weary years of thought.
The starkest fights must still be fought
The most surprising songs be sung.

So wrote James Elroy Flecker. And here is a quotation from Rilke:

This is at bottom the only courage that is demanded of us: to have courage for the most strange, the most singular and the most inexplicable that we may encounter. That mankind has in this sense been cowardly has done life endless harm: the experiences that are called "visions," the whole so-called "spirit world," death, all these things that are so closely akin to us, have by daily parrying been so crowded out of life, that the senses with which we could have grasped them are atrophied. To say nothing of God . . .

The holistic world view implies that the Whole is living Mind and Intelligence working as a vast and complex Unity. We may understand that everything is in vibration on ever subtler frequency rates, earth matter representing the lowest, densest vibration. Jacob's Ladder may be conceived as representing ever higher frequencies leading to the God Source and the inconceivably high vibration of the Spiritual Sun. And all these frequencies are present everywhere, though our senses can only apprehend the material.

We have grasped that Planet Earth is indeed a living creature, part of the vital organism of the solar system. The Sun compares with the heart center, and each of the planets is like one of the endocrine glands. When in our microcosm of a body one of these goes sick, the whole body suffers and is ill and we have to do something about it. When one of the "glands" of the solar system goes dark and poisoned, silent and sick, must we not expect that the Higher Intelligence will take action? Humanity, as we have seen, has been given free will which must be respected. But do we really expect that the higher worlds will therefore stand by and watch a planet destroy its web of life? There is a limit to toleration. The most liberal-minded parent would intervene if the children on July 4th or Guy Fawkes Night decided to build a bonfire in the drawing room! The parallel is valid. At *that* point parental authority would intervene. Mankind cannot be allowed to damage the holistic life structure of the solar system as a psycho-spiritual organism.

Recognize that disasters do not interfere with freedom. They stage dramatic situations with which we have to deal. And we know that the prophecies are warnings of what could happen but can nevertheless be avoided if we see light and amend our ways. This is apocalyptic talk. But always remember that the apocalyptic vision is not merely talking disaster. It recognizes that "after the tribulation cometh the Son of Man upon the clouds with power and a great glory and the trumpeting of angels." It is the cleansing, making way for the new dawn, the passing out of the Dark Age into the beginning of a new Golden Age.

This does *not* simply mean that we need not do anything about it since God is going to rescue us! Such thinking is simplistic to a degree. We are acknowledging the reality of levels of intelligence far higher than our own, which are all factors in the great living Oneness that is the Universe. This planet of ours is precious beyond all words. We have seen it as a seed point for a universal impulse of renewal, the fulfillment of a divine experiment. It is not thinkable that all this can be allowed to be snuffed out by human folly. Holistic thinking about the coming New Age must allow for our direct relationship to higher intelligences in the Cosmos. This factor cannot be left out and it surely includes a supreme hope. Here are our real allies with whom we can work. Here is Factor X wholly ignored by politics, economics and social planning, and yet the salvation of humanity may turn on its recognition.

It is true that in the earlier years of the New Age movement, considerable stress was laid on UFO's and the possibilities of a lift-off by space ships and Divine Intervention to cleanse the planet. In his admirable new book *Emergence: the Rebirth of the Sacred*, David Spangler gives the story of his own spiritual development in the New Age awakening. It is a most readable and sane statement, in which he shows how far the emphasis has changed in recent years, so that the primary concern is now to learn ways in which the individual can bring about inner changes in character and personality.

This "transformational journey" is of vital importance in order to build human beings who can move with poise and courage through times of change. There is a sense of urgency that a sufficient number of people may achieve the inner step in conscious constructive direction and control. Yet a true balance must be maintained, since the transformed individual remains the instrument which can channel the power and wisdom of higher intelligences. Human freedom is always respected, and therefore we are called on to take the initiative and make ourselves worthy of cooperating in the cleansing operation. Every one is important, and it has been well said that "God plus one is a majority." In truth, it might be said that we have to make of ourselves the finely tempered steel with which the tip of Michael's spear is to be shod. Divine intervention involves man as a conscious instrument in cooperation with the beneficent intelligences who fill the living universe. These, indeed, are our chief allies, and they have no intention of allowing this beautiful planet to become an arid and poisoned desert.

We should give consideration to the communications given from high sources and received by the sensitives. Many are now available and more are coming through, all bearing out the same picture. Of course, there can be deception and illusion and we must "test the spirits." But to ignore this aspect is a grave mistake when mankind is faced with such apalling dangers.

Recently the TV film "The Day After" was shown, to picture the immediate effects of nuclear war. The next day, the following communication was received by a highly accredited sensitive.

You may rest assured that this will not happen—as the Higher Forces will not allow it to happen. There are now many high spirits on Earth who are helping to raise the general consciousness to the level of the Spiritual Hierarchy, drawing up humanity towards the supreme reality. This Great Power is one of Mercy and of Love, which is more powerful than those negative forces generated on earth. We of the Spiritual Hierarchy are ever watching over those who are in control of the nuclear warheads and can stop any further disasters. Hiroshima was to warn mankind of its futility. DO NOT FEAR. There are checks and balances in Universal Law which will keep mankind on a path of growth and development now, towards the Higher Realm of that Supreme Reality—a magnetic force drawing the Higher Self upward on a path of returning to the divine source.

And now for a quotation from Alice Bailey's "Discipleship in the New Age" given by "The Tibetan," the Master DK.

Initiation veils a secret and the revelation of that secret is imminent. It is concerned with a peculiar type of energy which can be induced at a moment of supreme tension. It is closely related to the "blinding light" which Saul of Tarsus saw on the road to Damascus, and the "Blinding Light" which accompanied the discharge of energy from the atomic bomb. The "Blinding Light" which ever accompanies true conversion and the light which is released by the fission of the atom are one and the same expression on different levels of consciousness and are definitely related to the processes and effects of initiation. When the aspirant prays in the New Invocation, "Let Light descend on Earth," he is invoking something which humanity will have to learn to handle.

The wild hope is that there cannot be a full-scale nuclear war because it will not be allowed. Furthermore, we may see the implications of the concept that Christ has taken over the etheric body of the Earth and is therefore present in every nuclear center. Do we honestly feel He can allow His power to be used in uncontrolled destruction of his creation? Is it not more probable that the pressing of the button will be the signal for a controlled and vast demonstration of light filling the heavens? We live in a world infinitely strange and wonderful, and a kind of world initiation may be brought about.

We are challenged to lift our thinking and see that we have a major role to play in the transformation and redemption of the planet. Here is the true vision of the future—that we have reached the stage in evolution where we can recognize our true humanity and take that leap in consciousness into holistic thinking, which will lead us through into the New Age. A culture which has lost the "sense of the future" is bound to decline.

With holistic thinking, we recover the sense of purpose and direction in life and are filled with the ardor brought by a sense of the Future into which we are building. This gives the main spur for our working to achieve inner change in ourselves.

The staging of Operation Redemption implies that on the higher planes, the great oceans of life, thought and being work in a sublime harmony with the Divine Law and that the decree has gone out that all which causes disharmony shall be dissolved.

Let us close with a passage from the book *The Shining Brother* by Laurence Temple. It claims to be from St. Francis, speaking to one who had an earlier incarnation as his friend "Brother Lawrence."

The time hath come when the mysteries of the age shall be revealed to all who desire light upon their path, that they may approach the center of all Power and Life. For a new spirit is within the world and man throweth off his leading strings and will no longer follow blindly the blind leaders. He will accept instruction only from those who can perceive the Invisible and hear the Unspoken Word, who are filled with the Spirit and who speak with Inner Knowledge and have escaped from the bondage of creeds and the inherited beliefs of past generations. For the soul of man requireth freedom for the growth of the new age and strength to carry the burden of greater responsiblities. Therefore upon many will be poured forth the gifts of the Spirit, that light may penetrate the darkness and humanity be reborn nearer to the Divine Image. This is a Day of Days when many forces meet and much is shattered in the impact; yet in the Infinite Mind is the Supreme Thought, the creative urge towards perfection, and we who dwell in the Eternal Harmony are at one with these vast waves of Power, and all our being is given to this invincible direction of the thought forms of God . . . The Creative Power floweth through all, and each is a partaker in the Divine Plan and giveth that which he hath to the Universal Heritage.

Such is the scale of events we are experiencing and the meaning of the age we live in. Here is the supreme hope beyond tribulation. Let us hold to it, that in the darkness it may shine like a beacon. For there is Joy ahead, if now in the hour of darkness we can reach up into the Light.

We will close with a poem by F. C. Happold, the author of the well-known books on mysticism.

A wind has blown across the world
And tremors shake its frame,
New things are struggling to their birth

And naught shall be the same.
The earth is weary of its past
Of folly, hate and fear.
Beyond a dark and stormy sky
The dawn of God is near.

A wind is blowing through the earth
A tempest loud and strong,
The trumpets of the Christ the King
Thunder the skies along
The summons to a high crusade
Calling the brave and true
To find a New Jerusalem
And build the world anew.

This chapter began with a quotation, and I shall end with words from that quotation which I urge you to remember in all that you do.

I AM HERE, WITHIN THEE, I, THE LIVING GOD.

That alone will bring the New Day on Earth.

Appendix I
A Prayer for Peace

LEAD ME FROM DEATH TO LIFE, FROM FALSEHOOD TO TRUTH
LEAD ME FROM DESPAIR TO HOPE, FROM FEAR TO TRUST
LEAD ME FROM HATE TO LOVE, FROM WAR TO PEACE
LET PEACE FILL OUR HEART, OUR WORLD, OUR UNIVERSE.

This Prayer has been offered in a pamphlet put out by the Schumacher Society and the World Disarmament Campaign. In it this statement is made:

> *The root of war is fear. It is fear which initiates our dependence on weapons. It is fear which provokes us to develop systems of manipulation and greed, creating occasions of war. It is fear that constantly animates the arms race. It is fear that fuels lust for power. And it is fear that events have gone too far, that it is now "too late," that so often imprisons a creative, life-saving response.*

> *To combat fear and free us from this feeling of helplessness we need to add a different dimension—a dimension of global prayer and positive meditation for world peace. This will be a prayer to combat fear and a meditation to implant trust, a prayer for the sane use of resources, for the uplifting of the downtrodden and for the establishment of peace on earth.*

> *The aim is to organize a world vigil that will focus the will of people from every race and creed and denomination: two minutes a day,*

wherever you are, at midday your time . . . thus forming a chain of hours around the globe that will not be broken until these aims have been achieved.

One need not be a member of a church or spiritual organization to contribute. Prayer goes by many names. Positive thought itself is a form of prayer.

We believe in the power of prayer. Devote a few minutes every day (at midday) to prayer and meditation, so that the positive energy released in this way by countless minds across the Earth will make fear retreat and allow room for hope and positive action.

This kind of prayer will have immense power. The same power as that of air. Air is everywhere. Even though it is not visible, without it we cannot survive. By offering deep and total prayer individually and collectively in every country, we can change the atmosphere and inspire positive thinking.

****

Peace cannot be kept by force.
It can only be achieved by understanding.
(Albert Einstein)

Appendix II
The Lamplighter Movement

It would be fitting to tell the story of the founding of this movement and what led up to it. It all began from the inspiration of Wellesley Tudor-Pole, who was undoubtedly one of the great seers and adepts of this epoch. Those who have read his books, *The Silent Road*, *A Man Seen Afar* (far memories of the life of Jesus) and *Writing on the Ground*, will realize the scale of his vision and personality. Rosamond Lehmann has recently published an enchanting collection of his letters to her, under the title *Letters to Alexias*. They are written with his usual wit and perception and are a treasure house of wisdom, throwing light on many aspects of the spiritual awakening in our time. Among the many subjects touched upon is the Lamplighter Movement at its inception.

It grew in direct descent out of the Big Ben Silent Minute, launched at Tudor-Pole's initiative, in the dark days of 1940. Winston Churchill and George VI rose to the idea with enthusiasm and it was taken up by BBC, with the result that millions of freedom-lovers the world over united in silent prayer for protection of this Island during the striking of Big Ben at 9 p.m. The striking of Big Ben was discontinued in 1961 after twenty-one years. Then Tudor-Pole received another inner direction from the High Source, giving what he described as an imperative request that *light should replace sound*. Our unseen allies in the higher spheres required that small permanently burning lights should be lit and dedicated, ideally in an upper room so that they would shine out into the world. "T. P." stressed the importance of "repeatedly renewed intent" in dedicating the lights. They were to be amber, to represent the Spiritual Sun, the source of life and the Christ Impulse working down into the obscurity of matter. They could be an oil lamp or candle, but more conveniently a small 15 watt electric bulb. We are told that what happens is that the little light, combined with the dedicated intent, prayer and meditation, draws down a response from the next level of life and being. This usually takes the form of the creation of an answering light within the etheric counterpart of the room or center where the material point of light has been kindled. This then begins to cast its healing and inspiring glow across the dark areas of the Borderland, that region into which souls pass immediately after release from the body at death. A chain of interlacing events is set going, and focal centers of light then begin to multiply, not only in the Borderland itself, but up and up. Something like a spiritual lighthouse is established.

For us, the kindling of the light with dedicated and renewed intent is an outer gesture of interior purpose, demonstrating that here is a house in which prayer and meditation are rising. It creates a spiritual focus within our lives. It will often be in a sanctuary but can be in any convenient room or place, and ideally it should be perpetually burning. If it has to be extinguished, it should be rededicated on lighting again. Many have found, and particularly those who live alone, that the light brings a mysterious sense of peace and healing and of a beneficent presence. Yet we must always remember that our initiative is welcomed by the invisible worlds, because it makes possible a corresponding kindling of light on the spiritual plane. Thus the movement will be immensely larger than it appears on Earth and, once begun on the ethereal plane, may grow into a great network. Though we have a considerable mailing list, there is no means of knowing how widely it has spread. We hear of lights lit in many parts of the world.

Our first light was kindled in the very heart of England, at At-

tingham, om Midsummer Day 1964. I quote a personal letter from
T. P. written to me shortly after the Lamplighter Movement had
been launched:

> *For a long time past human consciousness and feeling have been*
> *plunging more and more deeply into the darkness of materialism.*
> *The din and complexities of modern life have shattered faith in the*
> *spiritual simplicities and their power to heal and to save. The furi-*
> *ous and uncontrolled Winds of Darkness strive to extinguish what*
> *Light is left in our outer World, to such an extent that Man has lost*
> *his belief in the very existence of Light itself and its power to heal,*
> *to inspire and to raise the level of moral standards. Even such a*
> *seemingly modest effort as is represented by the acts and the intent*
> *of the Lamplighters, possesses a promise for the future, of import*
> *far beyond our human comprehension. Even the symbolism itself*
> *helps the mind of ordinary men and women to begin to Look Up and*
> *to cease continually looking down into matter and into the gloom of*
> *past errors and delusions. A Cosmic mustard seed of immense po-*
> *tency and infinite promise was sown on Midsummer Day 1964.*

It should be stressed that this is not a cult or "movement" in
the sense that it carries any obligation of membership. There is no
dogma and it conflicts with no other belief. Lamplighters may
indeed feel themselves to be "members one of another" in a fel-
lowship on an inner plane. It is purely an outward gesture of
inner intent and commitment and is a symbol representing the
inner illumination to be achieved within mind and heart.

It will be sensed from what was written in the chapter on "Michael and All Angels" that the Lamplighter Movement has the
blessing of the Great Archangel and takes its place in the great
struggle between the Light and the forces of negation and darkness. Here is the suggested Prayer for the Dedication of a Light. It
could be used at the first kindling or at any appropriate occasion
thereafter.

I kindle this little light on the earth plane.
I dedicate it to the service of the Spirit.
I guard and cherish this flame as a living symbol,
  and an act of faith in the reality of the Powers of Light.

May the Beings from Higher Worlds see this flame
  and kindle its counterpart on the ethereal plane.
May this ethereal light be a channel for the inflow
  of healing powers of the spirit.
May the Love of Christ permeate this building
  and protect it, warming the hearts and
enlightening the understanding of all who
  live in it or enter it.

May the Being whom we know as Michael,
  Standard Bearer of the Christ, Wielder of
  the Sword of Light, use this offering, linking it
  with all those who have lit the light.
May the peace and healing spread through
  the world and the regions of the Borderland.

All Lamplighters are integrally part of the great network of Light Centers spreading across Britain and the world. It is like the flow of electricity from the generators and through transformers which reduce the voltage so that it may shine in little bulbs, or the flowing of the blood through the great arteries to the tiny capillaries. The little amber lights help to evoke the spiritual light. This indicates the increased significance of the Lamplighter Movement in this time of tension. First came the Big Ben Silent Minute and the wall of world prayer which protected our country in time of peril. Then came the Lamplighters after Big Ben had ceased to strike on BBC. Now comes what may be another imperative request from High Sources, that we do all that we can to strengthen the Grid of Light Centers against the moment (which may be soon) when it is really to be used. In such a network the smallest, humblest links are of first importance.

Thus the Lamplighter Movement now takes its place in an immensely bigger operation of activating light centers throughout the country to do their full part in carrying the energies of the Archangel Michael in the moment of renewal. This is a world event.

The time has come to give a renewed impetus to the Lamplighter Movement. Its importance now is greater than ever. New indications come from high sources that the physical lights, dedicated with prayer, are vitally important in the battle which is now joined between the powers of darkness and the Light. Across the world, the lights should be lit in homes which have allied themselves with Michael and his angelic powers. If Lamplighters take the initiative in making the movement known to others who might support it, the lights will proliferate, and the response from the Beyond will be very real. Those who wish to be on our mailing list as Lamplighters and receive the periodical "Letter to Lamplighters" should write to Wrekin Trust, Marbury House, St. Owen St., Hereford HR1 2PR, England, marking the envelope "Lamplighter Movement." (A donation for postage is welcomed.)

To quote the closing lines from T. S. Eliot's *Choruses from the Rock:*

> *And when we have built an altar to the*
> *invisible Light, we may set thereon the little*
> *lights for which our bodily vision is made.*
> *And we thank Thee that darkness reminds us of light.*
> *O Light Invisible, we give Thee thanks for Thy great glory.*

Bibliography

Chapter 1   A Holistic World View
              The Tao of Physics, Fritjof Capra (Wildwood & Fontana).
Chapter 2   The Quickening of the Spirit
              Within Is The Fountain, Leonora Nichols (C. W. Daniel).
Chapter 3   The Cosmic Christ in the New Age
              Cosmic Consciousness, R. M. Bucke (Putnam).
              Writing on the Ground, W. Tudor-Pole (Neville Spearman).
              Occult Science: An Outline, Rudolf Steiner (Rudolf Steiner Press).
              Christianity as Mystical Fact, Rudolf Steiner (Rudolf Steiner Press).
              The Risen Christ & The Etheric Christ, Alfred Heidenreich (Rudolf Steiner Press).
Chapter 4   Thoughts on the Second Coming
              The Reappearance of the Christ, Alice Bailey (Lucis Trust).
              Revelation: The Birth of a New Age, David Spangler (Findhorn).
              The Book of Revelation, Alfred Heidenreich (Floris Books).
              The True Nature of the Second Coming, Rudolf Steiner (Rudolf Steiner Press).
              Le Milieu Divin, Teilhard de Chardin (Collins).

Chapter 5   Michael and All Angels
            The Kingdom of the Gods, Geoffrey Hodson (Rudolf
            Steiner Press).
            The Mission of the Archangel Michael, Rudolf Steiner.
            and Another Great Angel, Stewart Easton (Steiner
            Press).

Chapter 7   Finding the Inner Teacher
            The Spirit of Counsel, Mary Swainson (Neville Spear-
            man).
            The Impersonal Life, Joseph Benner (C. A. Willing).
            Challenge, Frédéric Lionel (Neville Spearman).
            Imitation of Christ, Thomas à Kempis (Fontana).
            Into God, Robert Coulson (John Murray).

Chapter 8   Exploring Inner Space
            Man or Matter, Ernst Lehrs (Faber).
            The Plant Between Earth and Sun, George Adams and
            Olive Whicher (Rudolf Steiner Press).
            Knowledge of Higher Worlds: How it is Achieved?, Ru-
            dolf Steiner (Rudolf Steiner Press).
            On Having No Head, Douglas Harding (Buddhist So-
            ciety).

Chapter 9   Essene Teachings and Huna Vision
            Essene Teachings From Enoch to the Dead Sea Scrolls,
            Edmond Szekely (C. W. Daniels).
            The Gospel of the Essenes, Edmond Szekely (C. W.
            Daniels).
            The Secret Science Behind Miracles, Max Freedom
            Long (Huna Research Publications).
            The Secret Science at Work, Max Freedom Long (Huna
            Research Publications).
            Growing Into Light, Max Freedom Long (Huna Re-
            search Publications).

Chapter 10 Festivals and Holy Places
The Light in Britain, Grace Cooke (White Eagle Publishing Co.).
The View Over Atlantis, John Michel (Garnstone).
The Pattern of the Past, Guy Underwood (Museum Press).
Needles of Stone, Tom Graves (Turnstone Press).
The Old Straight Track, Alfred Watkins (Abacus).
Spirit in Matter, L. Kolisko (Kolisko Archives, Rudolf Steiner Press).

Chapter 11 Man's Relation to the Animal Kingdom
Kinship With All Life, Boone (Harper and Row).
The Civilized Alternative, Jon Wynne-Tyson (Centaur Press).
Slaughter of the Innocents, Hans Ruesch (Futura).
Man as Symphony of the Creative Word, Rudolf Steiner (Rudolf Steiner Press).
Man and Animal, Herman Poppelbaum (Rudolf Steiner Press).
A New Zoology, Herman Poppelbaum (Rudolf Steiner Press).

Chapter 12 Alternative Lifestyle and the Holistic World View
The Essene Way—Biogenic Living, Edmond Szekely (C. W. Daniels).
Zen in the Art of Archery, Eugen Herrigel (Routledge, Kegan Paul).
Golf in the Kingdom, Michael Murphy (Gollancz).
The Alexander Principle, Dr. Wilfred Barlow (Gollancz).

Chapter 13 Operation Redemption
The Seventh Enemy, Ronald Higgins (Hodder & Stoughton).

The Six O'Clock Bus. A Guide to Armageddon and the New Age, Moira Timms (Turnstone Press).

The Quest for Gaia, Kit Pedler (Souvenir Press).

Secret of the Andes, Brother Philip (Neville Spearman).

The Shining Brother, Laurence Temple (Psychic Press).

Emergence—The Rebirth of the Sacred, David Spangler

SIR GEORGE TREVELYAN, Bt, M.A., is well known for this pioneering work in adult education, both as the principal of Attingham Park (1948-1971), and, in his retirement, as Founder, Director and now President of the Wrekin Trust, an educational charity concerned with the spiritual nature of man and the universe. He is an eloquent lecturer and an inspiring teacher, bringing to many subjects a freshness and originality of approach.

THE WREKIN TRUST arranges weekend and day conferences and courses, which are often the first opportunity for people interested in the same subject to meet others approaching it from a different point of view, attracting speakers of international repute.

Details from: The Wrekin Trust, Marbury House, St. Owen St., Hereford HR1 2PR, England.